First Grade
Math
with Confidence
Student Workbook

First Grade Math with Confidence

Student Workbook

KATE SNOW

WELL-TRAINED MIND PRESS

Table of Contents

This Student Workbook is only one component of *First Grade Math with Confidence*, and it is not meant to be used as a stand-alone workbook. The hands-on teaching activities in the Instructor Guide are an essential part of the program.

Circle the plate with more cookies.

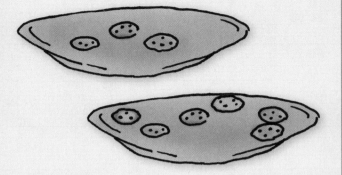 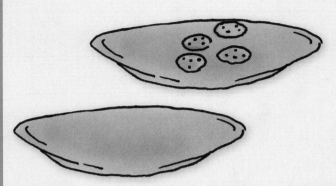

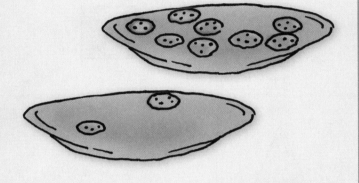 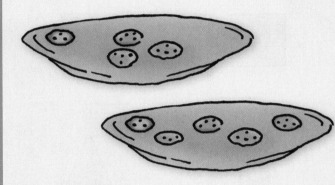

Circle the greater number in each pair.

 4   1   0

7   2   6   9

9   8   3   10

Trace the numbers.

1 2 3 4 5

6 7 8 9 10

X the shape that is different from the rest.

Circle the greater number in each pair.

(6) 3   5 8

9 8   4 6

9 10   7 0

Trace and copy.

1   2   3   4

5   6   7   8

9   10

Write the number that comes between each pair of numbers. Lesson 1.3B

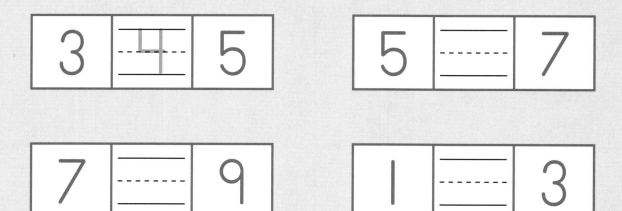

3 | 4 | 5   5 | ___ | 7

7 | ___ | 9   1 | ___ | 3

Color the left side of each shape yellow.
Color the right side of each shape red.

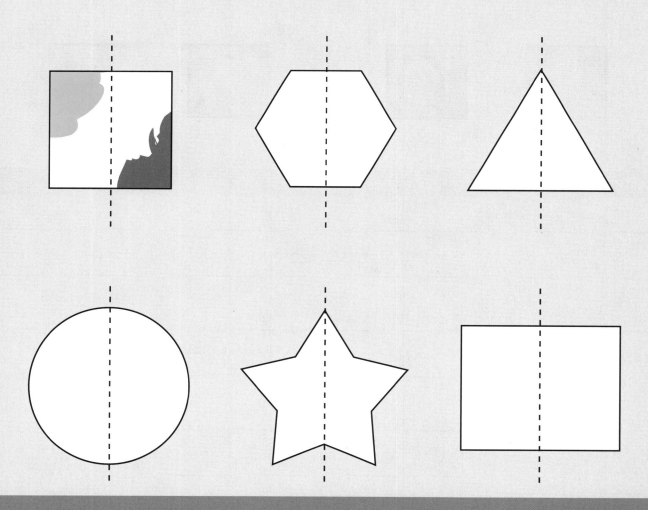

Color the cookies to complete the pattern.

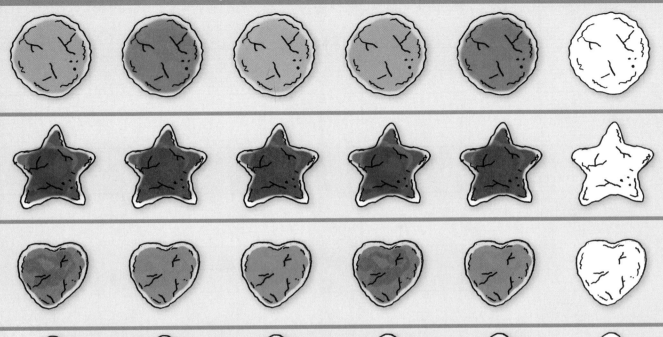

**Fill the outline with pattern blocks two different ways.
Write how many blocks you use.**

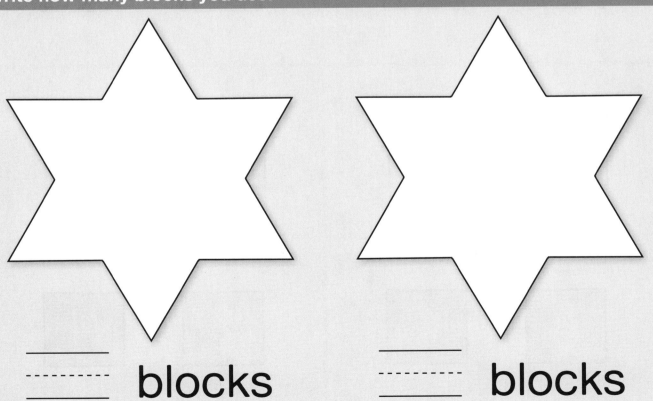

_____ blocks _____ blocks

1 2 3 4

5 6 7 8

9 10

Circle the greater number in each pair.

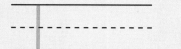

9 1 5 2

7 8 0 3

6 10 8 4

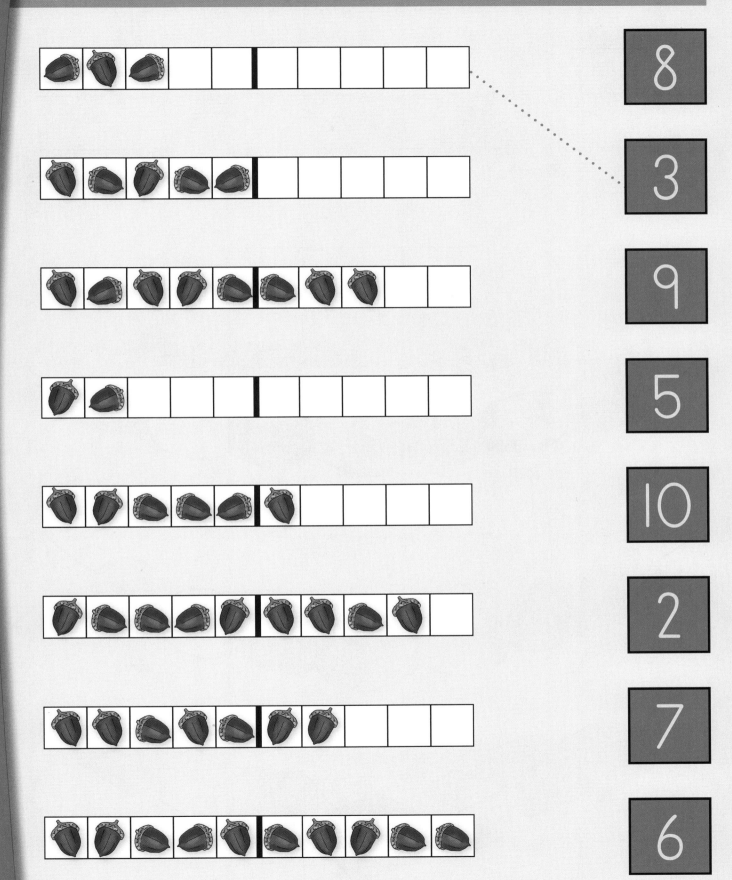

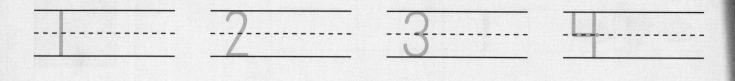

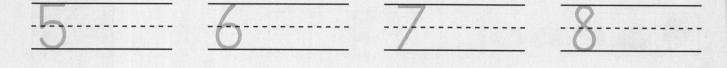

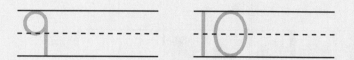

Color the beads to complete the pattern.

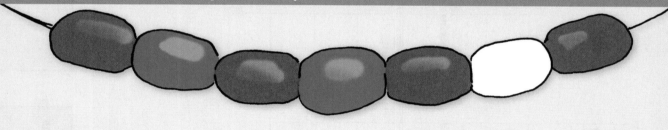

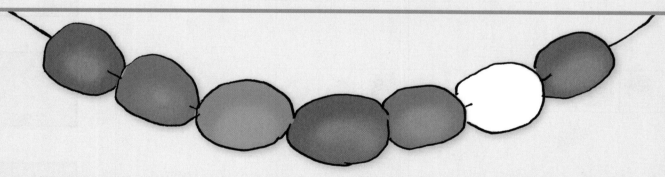

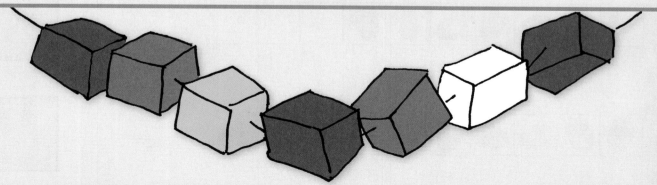

Match.

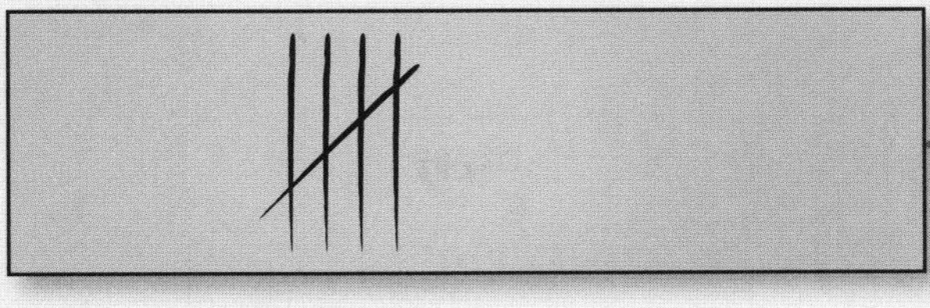

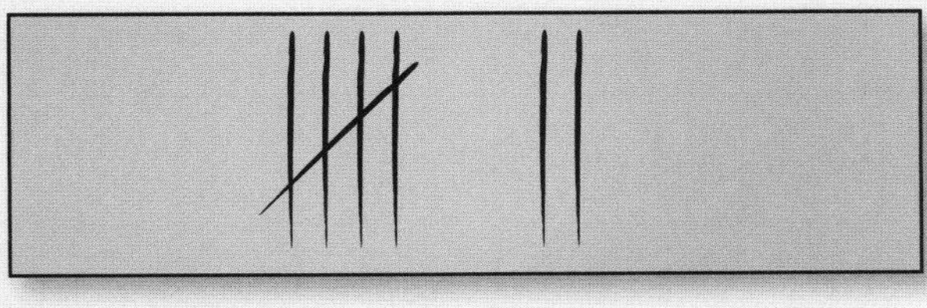

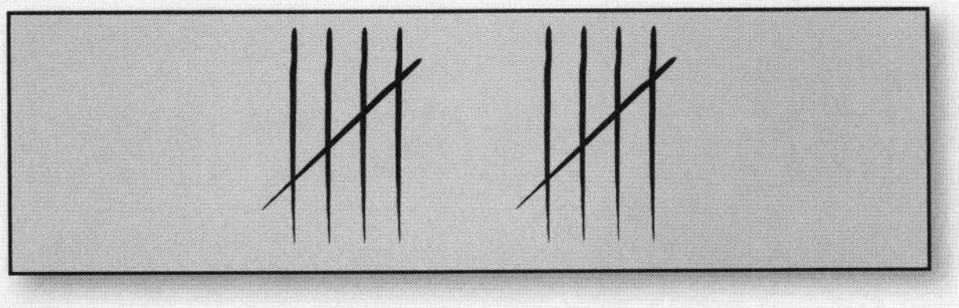

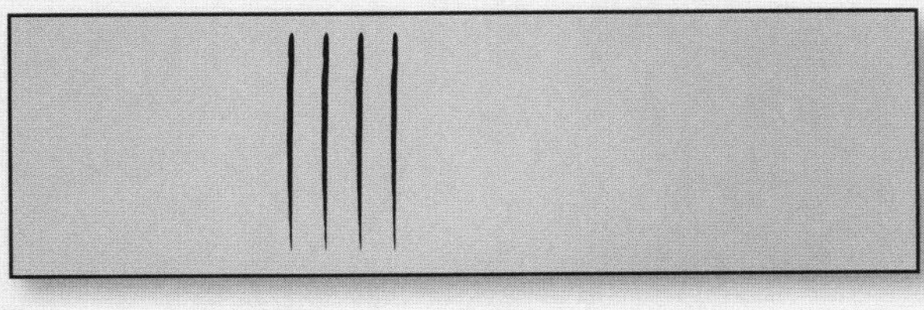

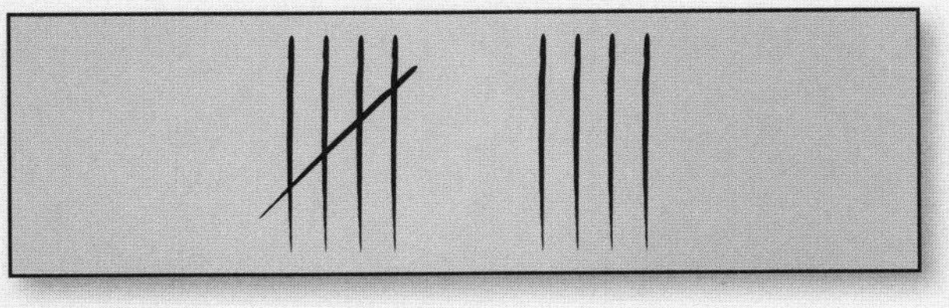

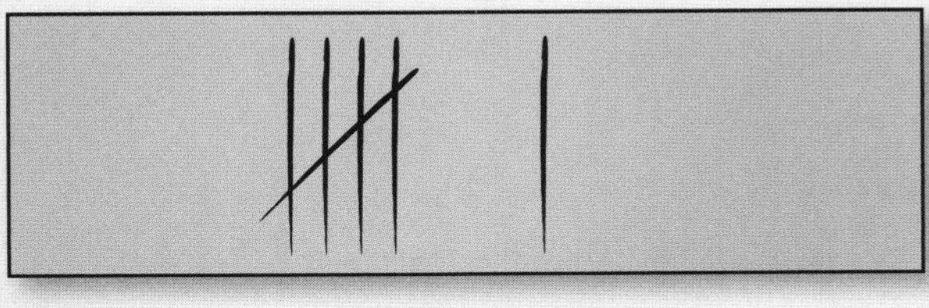

2

10

5

4

7

1

6

9

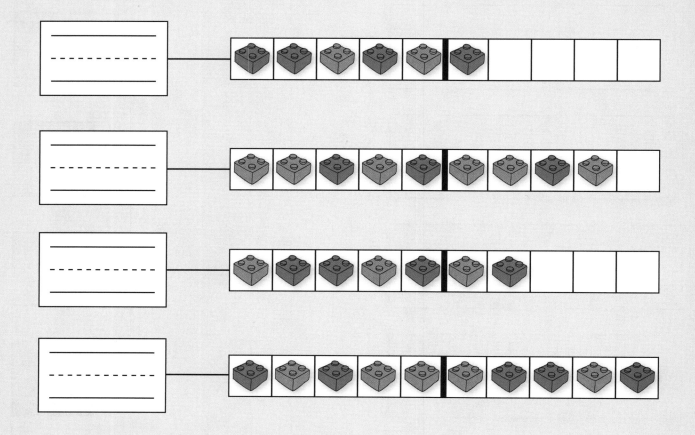

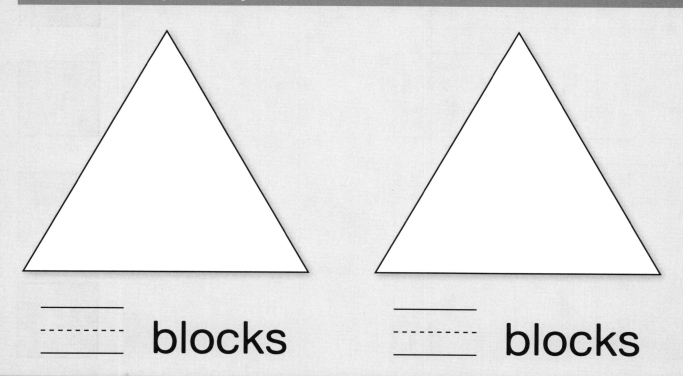

blocks

blocks

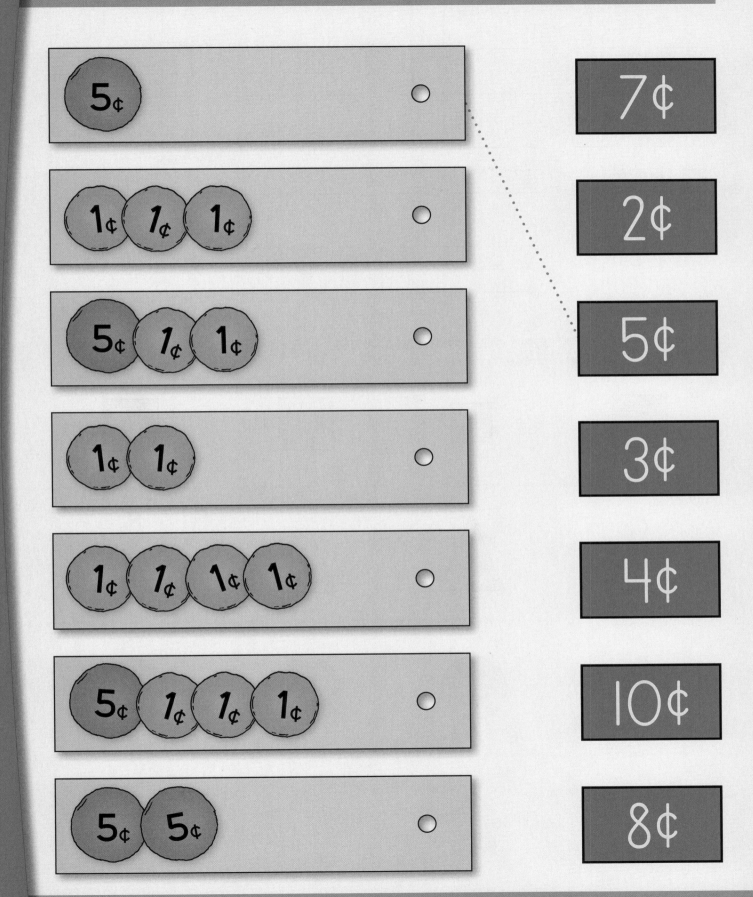

1   2   3   4

5   6   7   8

9   10

X the shape that is different from the rest.

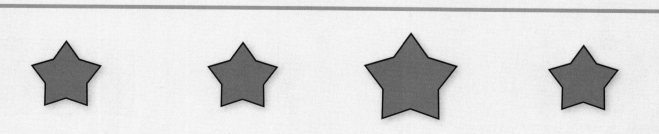

     Lesson 2.3B

Complete.

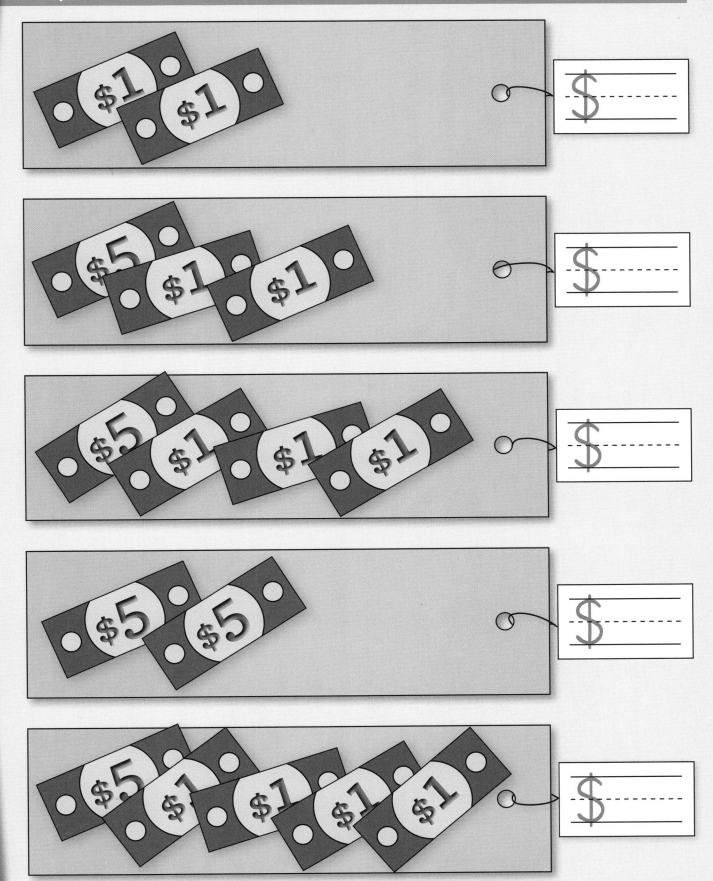

Write how many.

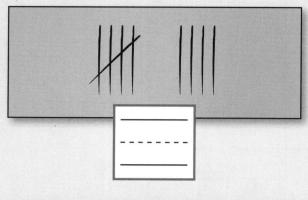

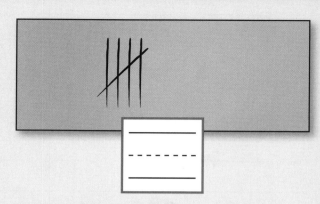

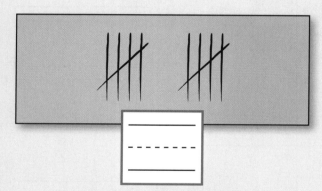

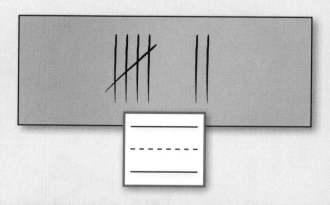

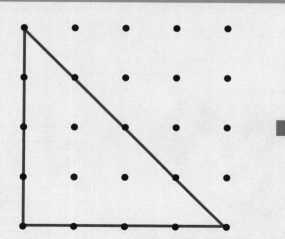

Copy the shape.

Complete.

5	5
2 + ___	4 + ___

5	5
___ + 0	1 + ___

5	5
___ + 5	3 + ___

Complete.

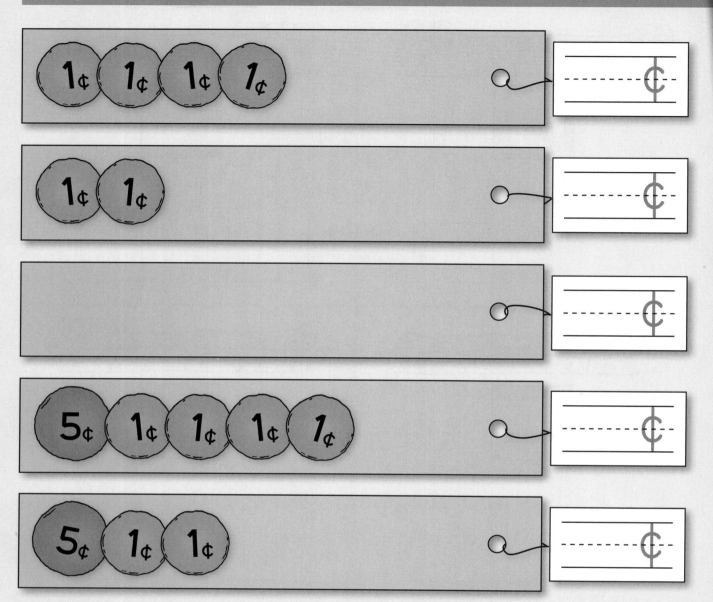

Copy the shape.

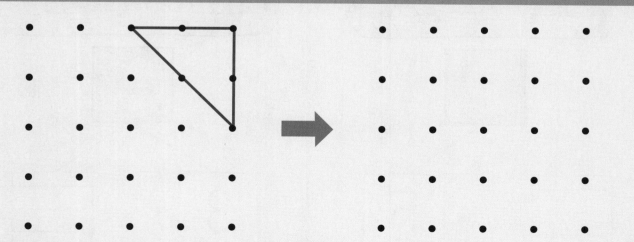

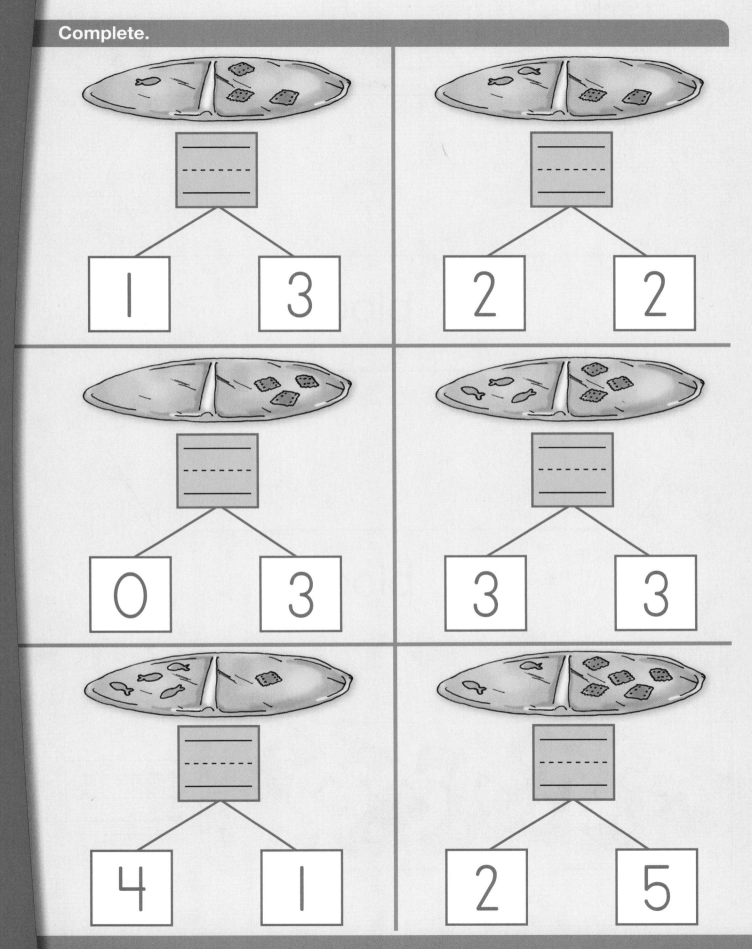

**Fill the outline with pattern blocks two different ways.
Write how many blocks you use.**

_____ blocks

_____ blocks

Complete.

$ _____

Lesson 3.2B

Complete.

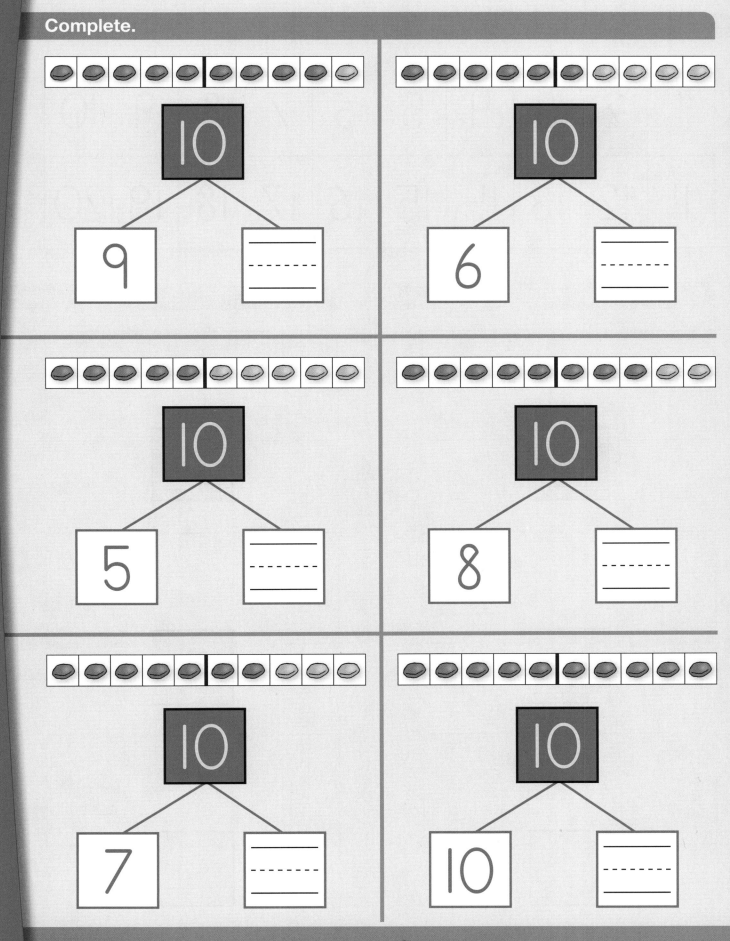

Color the numbers you say when you count by 2s.

1	2	3	4	5	6	7	8	9	10
11	12	13	14	15	16	17	18	19	20

Draw tallies to match.

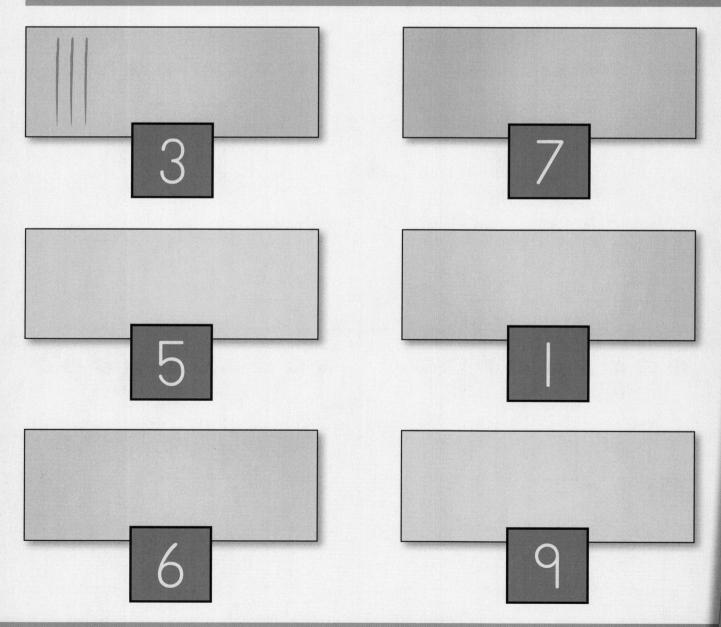

3

7

5

1

6

9

Complete. Use the ten-frame at the top to help.

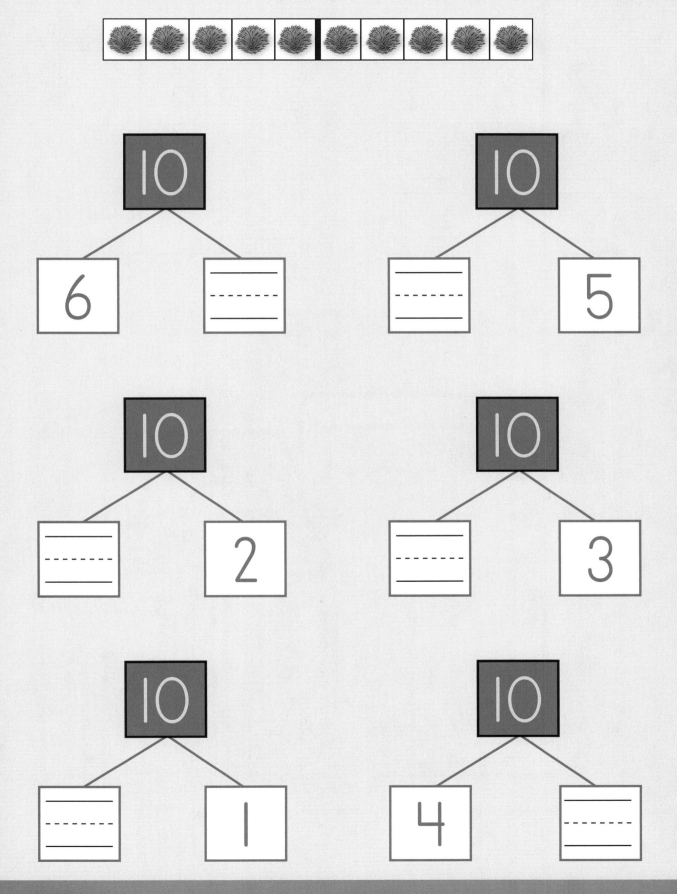

Write the numbers that come before and after each number.

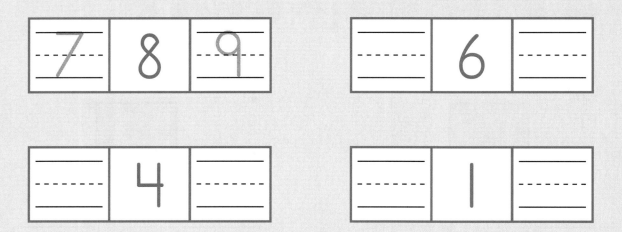

Complete the maze. Find the numbers in order from 1 to 10.

Lesson 3.4B

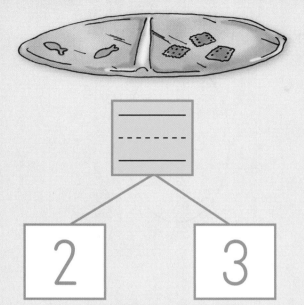

2	3

2 + 3 = _____

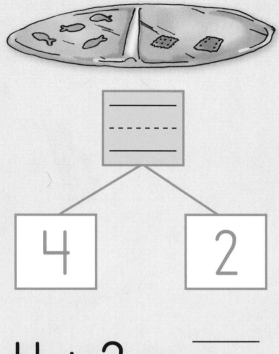

4	2

4 + 2 = _____

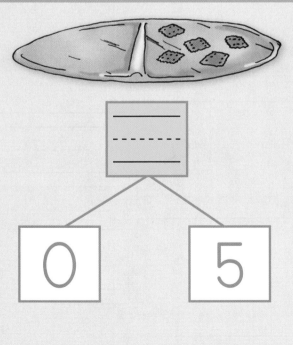

0	5

0 + 5 = _____

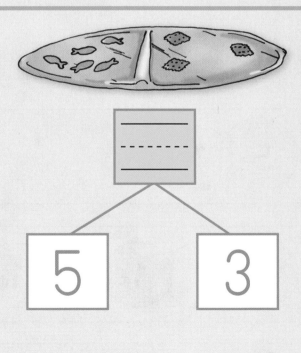

5	3

5 + 3 = _____

Color the left side of each shape yellow.
Color the right side of each shape red.

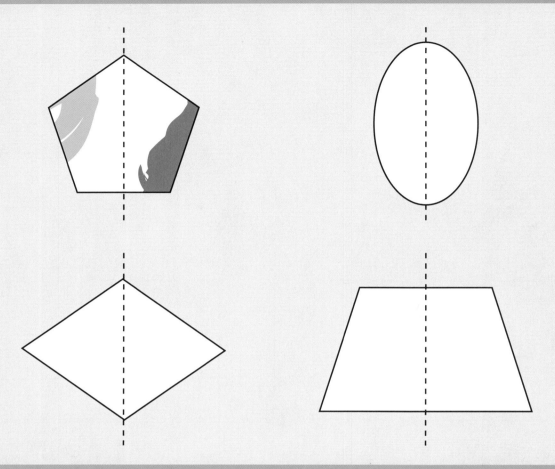

Complete.

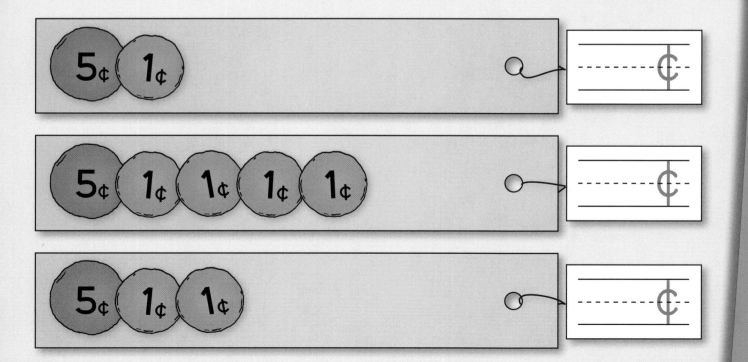

Lesson 4.1B

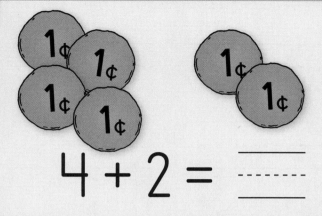

$4 + 2 =$ _____

$2 + 5 =$ _____

$6 + 1 =$ _____

$3 + 2 =$ _____

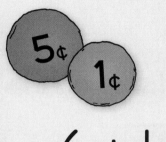

$7 + 1 =$ _____

$2 + 2 =$ _____

$3 + 1 =$ _____

$1 + 5 =$ _____

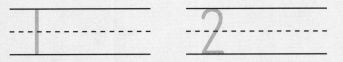

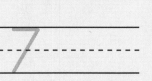
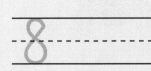
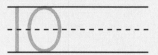

Complete.

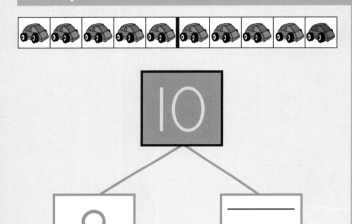

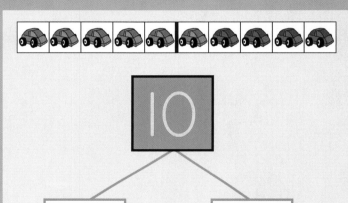

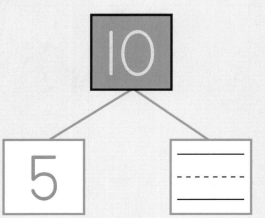

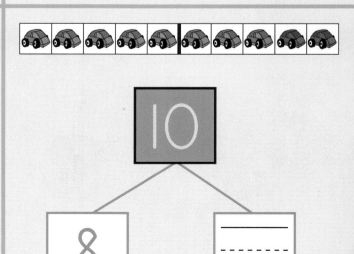

$8 + 1 =$ _____

$5 + 1 =$ _____

$6 + 1 =$ _____

$7 + 1 =$ _____

$8 + 2 =$ _____

$5 + 2 =$ _____

$6 + 2 =$ _____

$7 + 2 =$ _____

$8 + 0 =$ _____

$5 + 0 =$ _____

5
2 | _____

5
4 | _____

5
_____ | 0

5
_____ | _____

Write the number that comes before and after each number.

_____ 7 _____

_____ 3 _____

Complete.

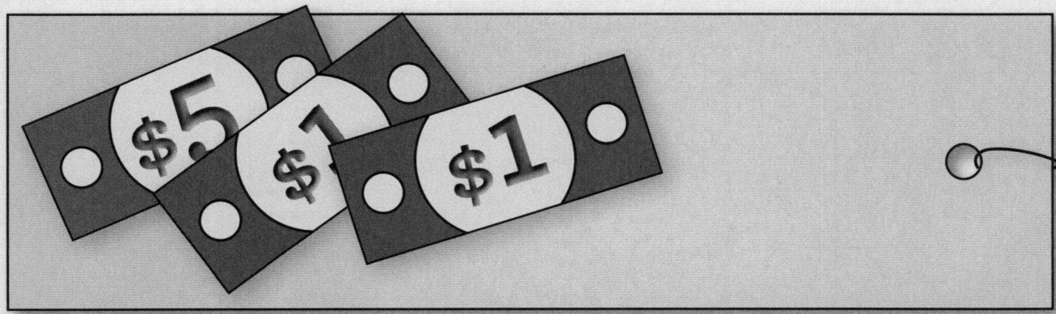

$5 $1 $1

$ _____

6 + 1	5	4 + 2
4 + 1	6	7 + 2
1 + 7	7	5 + 2
5 + 1	8	8 + 2
8 + 1	9	6 + 1
9 + 1	10	3 + 2

5   2

6   2

8   2

4   2

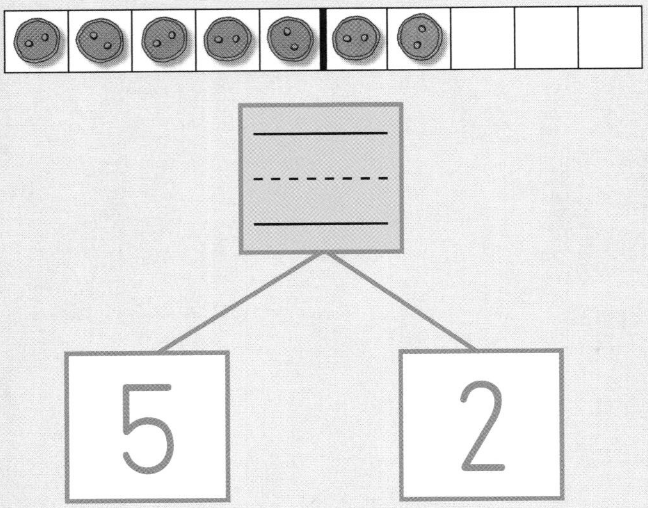

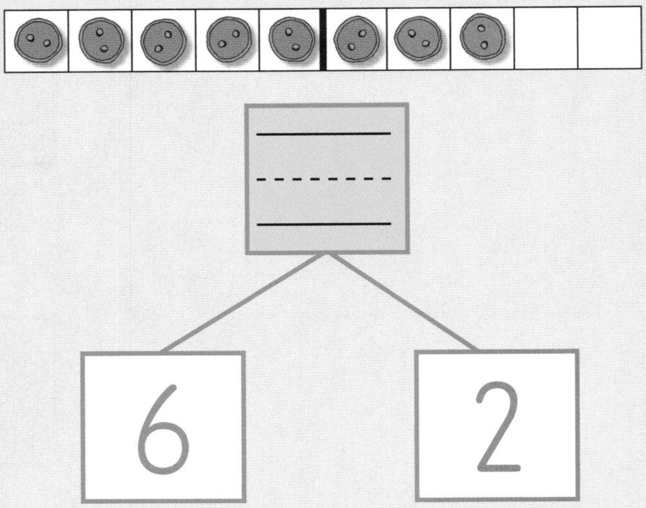

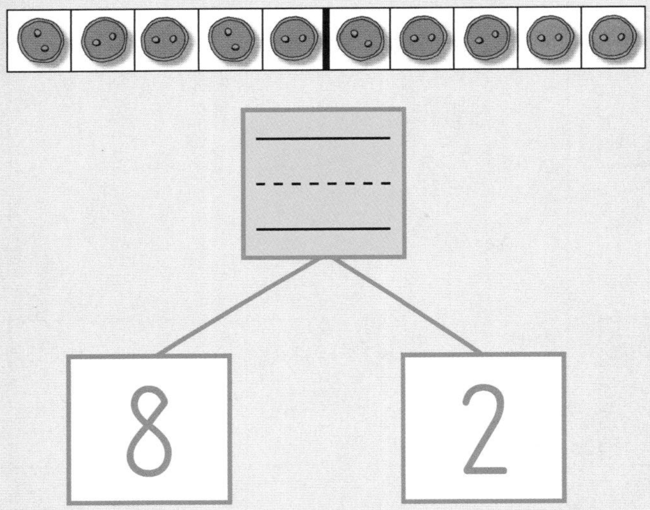

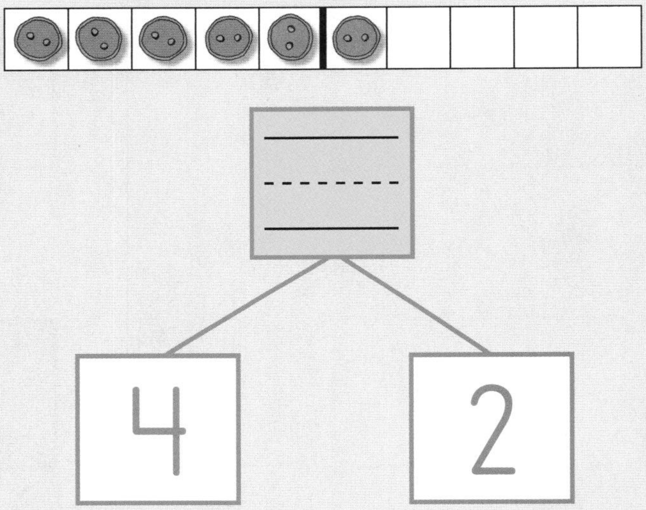

Copy the shape.

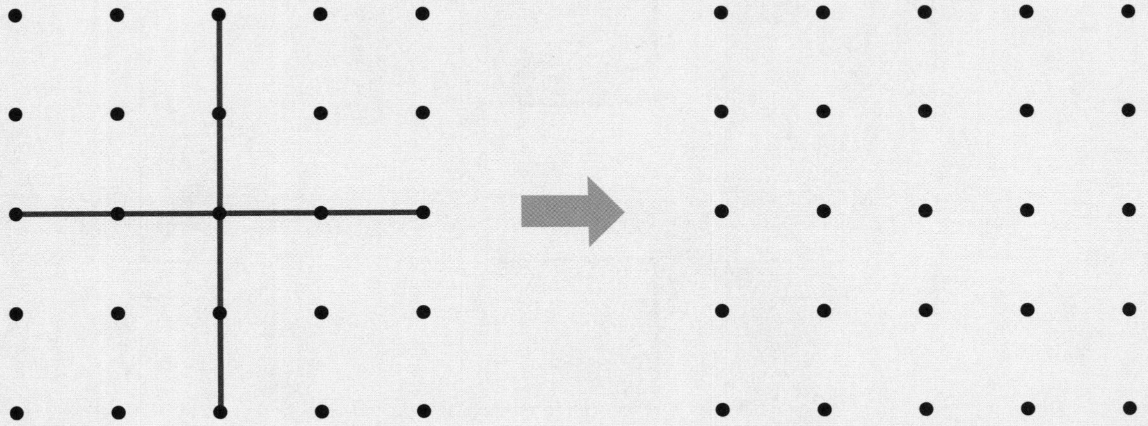

Addition Climb to the Top
Game Boards

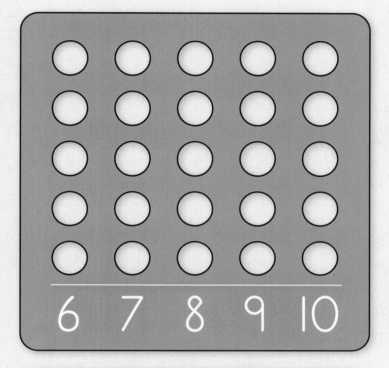

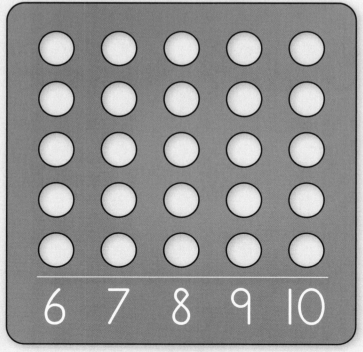

4 + 4 = _____

5 + 3 = _____

6 + 3 = _____

3 + 3 = _____

6 + 4 = _____

4 + 3 = _____

5 + 4 = _____

4 + 5 = _____

Count by 2s to continue the pattern.

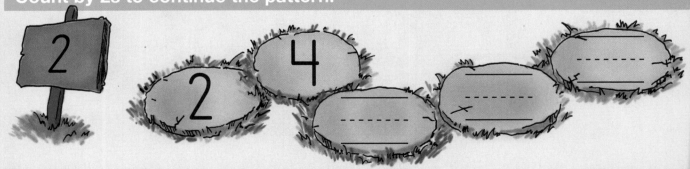

Complete.

$3 + 5 =$ _____ $4 + 4 =$ _____

$3 + 3 =$ _____ $4 + 5 =$ _____

$6 + 3 =$ _____ $6 + 4 =$ _____

Color the addition facts that equal the number in the star.

⭐ 7	⭐ 8	⭐ 9
$6 + 2$	$7 + 2$	$6 + 3$
$3 + 4$	$4 + 4$	$5 + 4$
$6 + 1$	$0 + 8$	$6 + 2$
$4 + 2$	$5 + 3$	$7 + 2$
$5 + 2$	$6 + 1$	$5 + 3$

Complete.

Match pairs that make 10.

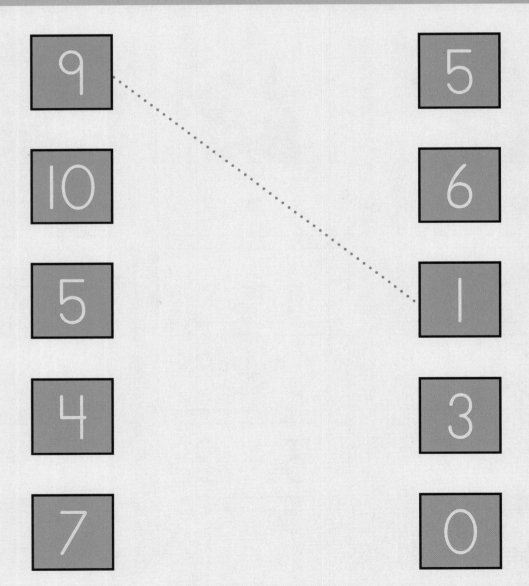

Complete.

4 + 4 = _____

5 + 3 = _____

5 + 4 = _____

3 + 6 = _____

3 + 3 = _____

3 + 4 = _____

6 + 1 = _____

4 + 4 = _____

Use the key to color the leaves.

Key
7 - red
8 - brown
9 - orange

0 + 8

6 + 1

5 + 4

7 + 2

2 + 6

5 + 2

5 + 3

9 + 0

Circle the greater number in each pair.

(8) 4   3 0

5 2   8 9

6 8   9 8

Complete.

$ _____

$ _____

4 + 3		4 + 5
	7	
6 + 3		3 + 4
	8	
5 + 3		3 + 6
	9	
5 + 4		3 + 5

Complete.

8 + 2 = _____   3 + 3 = _____

4 + 4 = _____   7 + 1 = _____

4 + 6 = _____   5 + 2 = _____

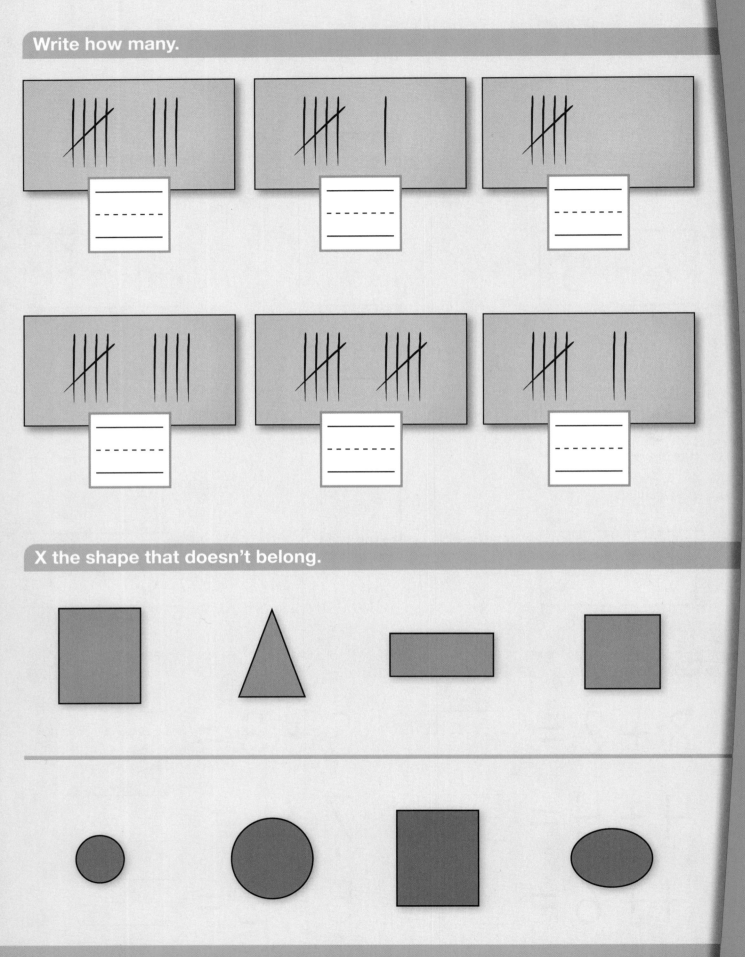

X the shape that doesn't belong.

9 + 1 = 10

___ + ___ = 10

___ + ___ = 10

___ + ___ = 10

___ + ___ = 10

___ + ___ = 10

___ + ___ = 10

___ + ___ = 10

Color the numbers you say when you count by 2s.

1	2	3	4	5	6	7	8	9	10
11	12	13	14	15	16	17	18	19	20
21	22	23	24	25	26	27	28	29	30

Color the flowers to complete the patterns.

Complete.

Lesson 6.1B

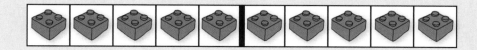

$8 + \underline{2} = 10$ $\qquad$ $\underline{} + 9 = 10$

$7 + \underline{} = 10$ $\qquad$ $\underline{} + 4 = 10$

$10 + \underline{} = 10$ $\qquad$ $\underline{} + 1 = 10$

$4 + \underline{} = 10$ $\qquad$ $\underline{} + 6 = 10$

$0 + \underline{} = 10$ $\qquad$ $\underline{} + 5 = 10$

8 + 2 = _____   3 + 3 = _____

4 + 4 = _____   7 + 1 = _____

4 + 6 = _____   5 + 2 = _____

Fill the outline with pattern blocks. Write how many blocks you use.

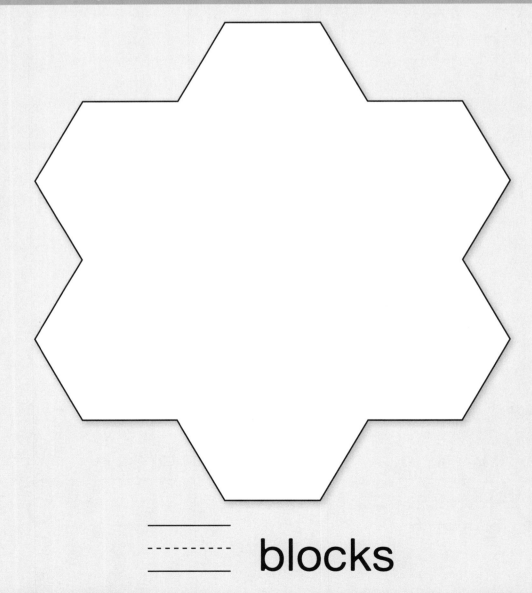

_____ **blocks**

Complete.

8 + 2 = :::::::::

3 + 3 = :::::::::

4 + 4 = :::::::::

7 + 1 = :::::::::

4 + 6 = :::::::::

5 + 2 = :::::::::

Color the addition facts that equal the number in the star.

7

| 6 + 2 |
| 3 + 4 |
| 6 + 1 |
| 4 + 2 |
| 5 + 2 |

8

| 7 + 2 |
| 4 + 4 |
| 0 + 8 |
| 5 + 3 |
| 6 + 1 |

9

| 6 + 3 |
| 5 + 4 |
| 6 + 2 |
| 7 + 2 |
| 5 + 3 |

Complete.

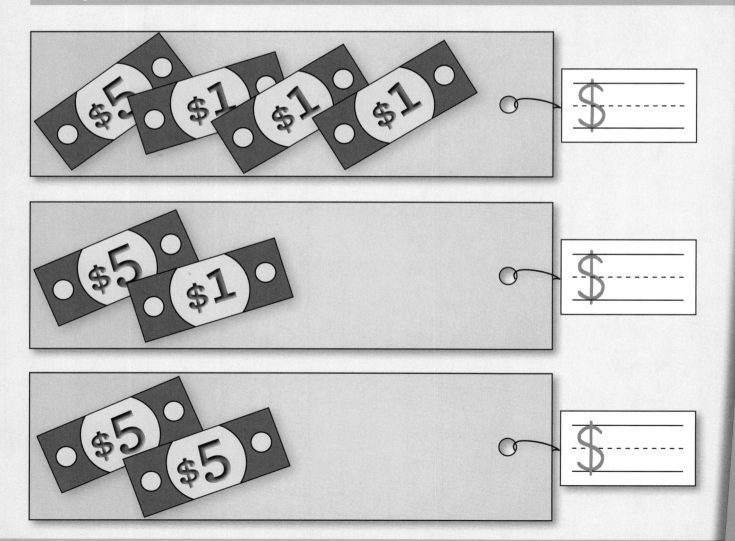

8 + 2		3 + 7
6 + 3	**8**	7 + 1
4 + 4	**9**	4 + 6
5 + 5	**10**	3 + 5

Complete.

7 + 2 = _____   8 + 0 = _____

4 + 5 = _____   9 + 1 = _____

4 + 3 = _____   6 + 2 = _____

3 + 3 = _____   3 + 6 = _____

Connect the numbers in order from 1 to 10.

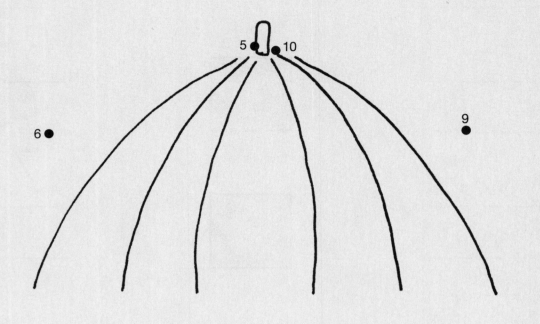

Copy the shape.

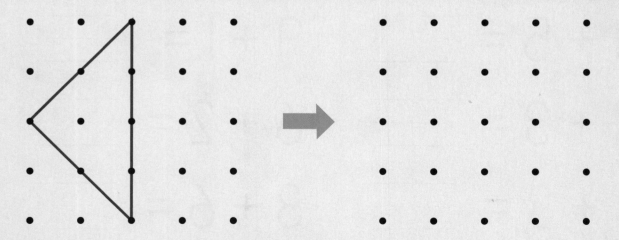

Color the circles. X the shapes that are not circles.

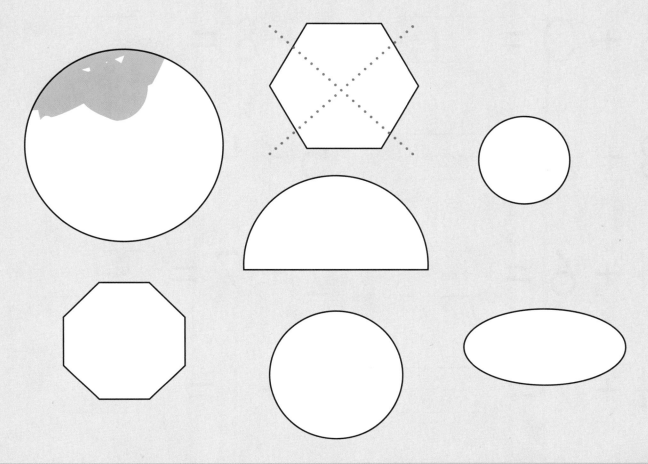

Draw a picture with straight lines and curved lines.

Complete.

6 + 0 = _____   1 + 8 = _____

3 + 2 = _____   5 + 4 = _____

4 + 6 = _____   2 + 7 = _____

4 + 2 = _____   5 + 1 = _____

1 + 6 = _____   7 + 0 = _____

Write the number that comes before and after.

Color the triangles. X the shapes that are not triangles.

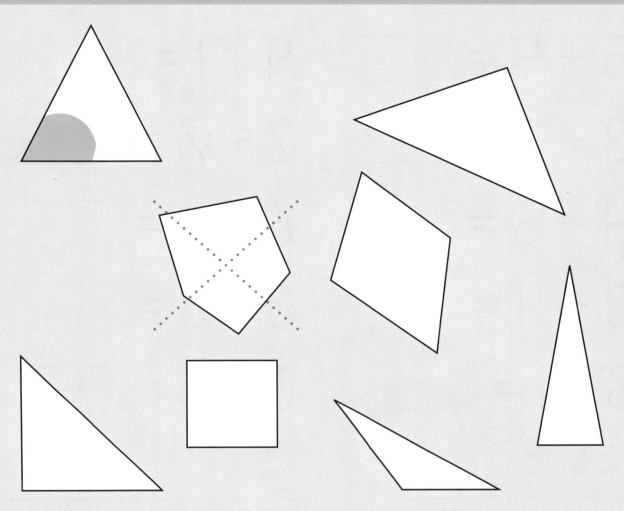

Connect the dots in order to make triangles.
Use a ruler to draw straight lines.

2 ●

1 ●   ● 3

● 2

1 ●

● 3

5 + 4 = _____   9 + 1 = _____

3 + 3 = _____   2 + 7 = _____

4 + 6 = _____   6 + 2 = _____

3 + 4 = _____   3 + 6 = _____

8 + 1 = _____   3 + 5 = _____

Color the numbers you say when you count by 2s.

1	2	3	4	5	6	7	8	9	10
11	12	13	14	15	16	17	18	19	20
21	22	23	24	25	26	27	28	29	30
31	32	33	34	35	36	37	38	39	40

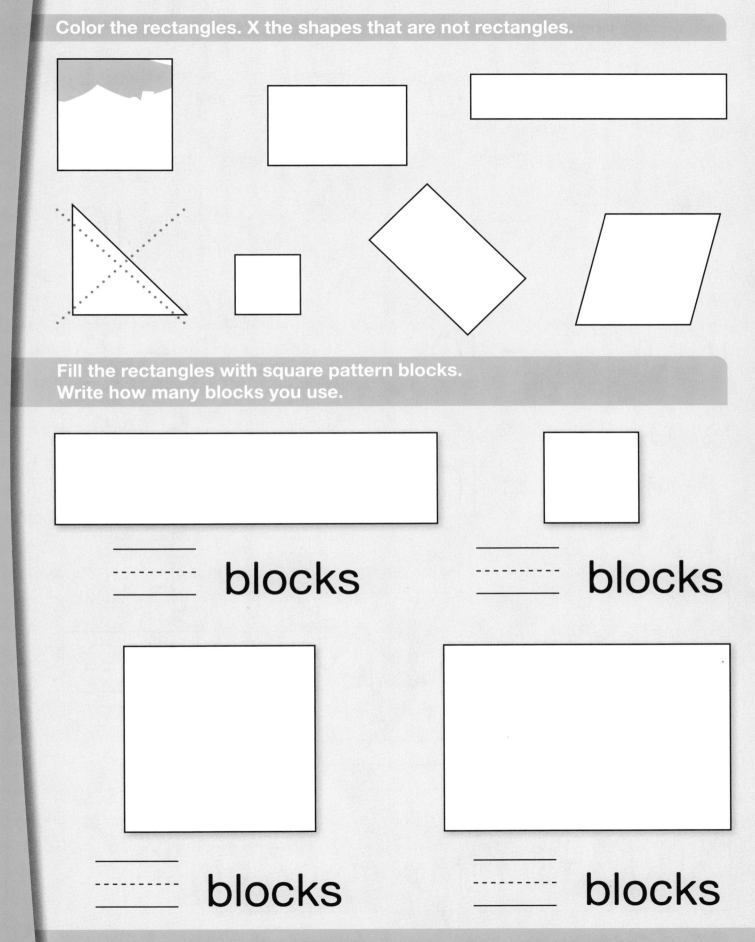

Fill the rectangles with square pattern blocks.
Write how many blocks you use.

_____ blocks

_____ blocks

_____ blocks

_____ blocks

8 + _____ = 10   _____ + 9 = 10

7 + _____ = 10   _____ + 2 = 10

10 + _____ = 10   _____ + 1 = 10

4 + _____ = 10   _____ + 5 = 10

Complete.

$ _____

$ _____

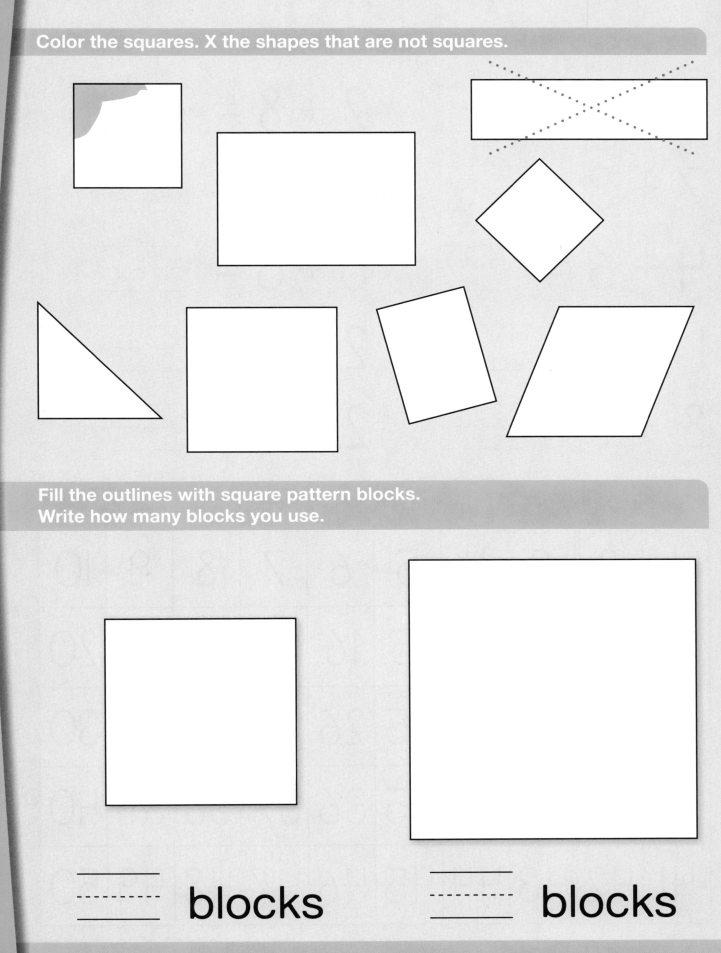

Fill the outlines with square pattern blocks.
Write how many blocks you use.

_____
- - - - - - - - blocks

_____
- - - - - - - - blocks

$4 + 4 =$ _____ $2 + 8 =$ _____

$7 + 3 =$ _____ $6 + 0 =$ _____

$4 + 6 =$ _____ $5 + 5 =$ _____

$1 + 5 =$ _____ $2 + 3 =$ _____

$8 + 1 =$ _____ $2 + 5 =$ _____

Color the numbers you say when you count by 5s.

1	2	3	4	5	6	7	8	9	10
11	12	13	14	15	16	17	18	19	20
21	22	23	24	25	26	27	28	29	30
31	32	33	34	35	36	37	38	39	40
41	42	43	44	45	46	47	48	49	50

Circle the sandwiches that are split in half.
X the sandwiches that are not split in half.

Draw a line that splits each shape in half.

4 + 4 = _____   6 + 2 = _____

6 + 3 = _____   5 + 5 = _____

6 + 4 = _____   2 + 2 = _____

1 + 4 = _____   4 + 3 = _____

3 + 3 = _____   2 + 8 = _____

Draw a picture that has a square, circle, and triangle in it.

Circle the pizzas that are split into fourths.
X the pizzas that are not split into fourths.

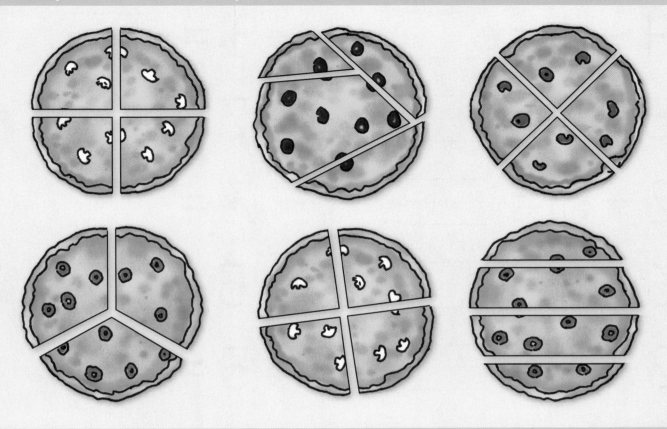

Draw lines that split each brownie into fourths.
Use a different way for each brownie.

Complete.

4 + 1 = _____   1 + 9 = _____

5 + 4 = _____   2 + 7 = _____

2 + 5 = _____   1 + 7 = _____

6 + 3 = _____   5 + 5 = _____

2 + 1 = _____   3 + 5 = _____

Match.

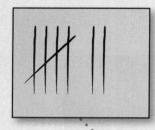  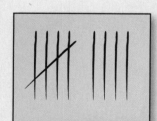 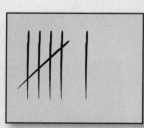

Draw a line of symmetry for each object.

1 + 1 = ...

0 + 2 = ...

2 + 2 = ...

2 + 4 = ...

3 + 3 = ...

4 + 6 = ...

4 + 4 = ...

3 + 5 = ...

5 + 5 = ...

2 + 8 = ...

X the shape that doesn't belong in each row.

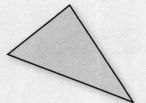 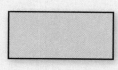

Match the congruent shapes.

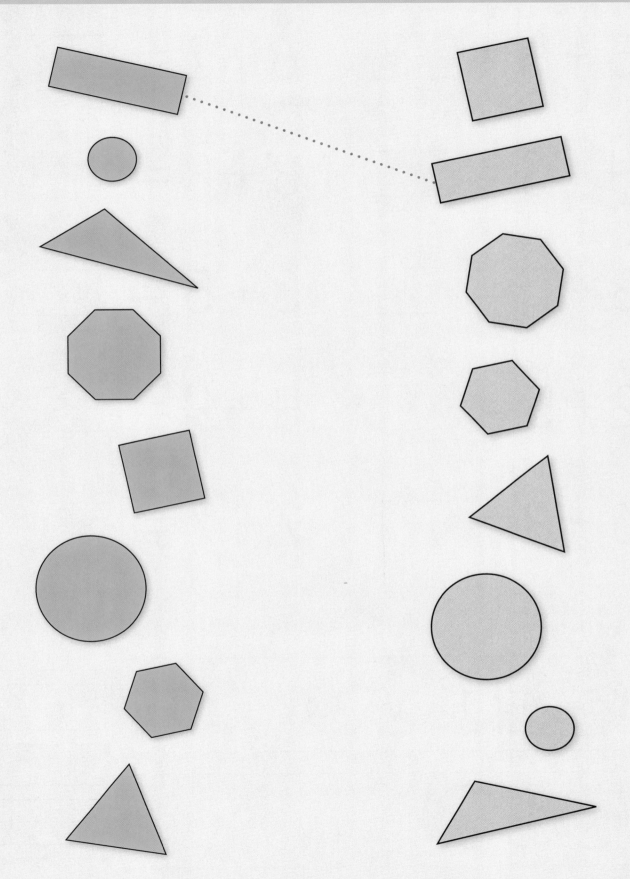

5 + 4 = _____   6 + 2 = _____

4 + 3 = _____   3 + 3 = _____

3 + 7 = _____   3 + 5 = _____

2 + 5 = _____   4 + 4 = _____

6 + 3 = _____   2 + 7 = _____

Complete.

$$9 - 1 = \underline{}$$

$$6 - 1 = \underline{}$$

$$7 - 1 = \underline{}$$

$$8 - 2 = \underline{}$$

$$10 - 2 = \underline{}$$

$$7 - 2 = \underline{}$$

$$8 - 1 = \underline{}$$

$$9 - 2 = \underline{}$$

$$6 - 2 = \underline{}$$

$$5 - 1 = \underline{}$$

Match pairs that make 10.

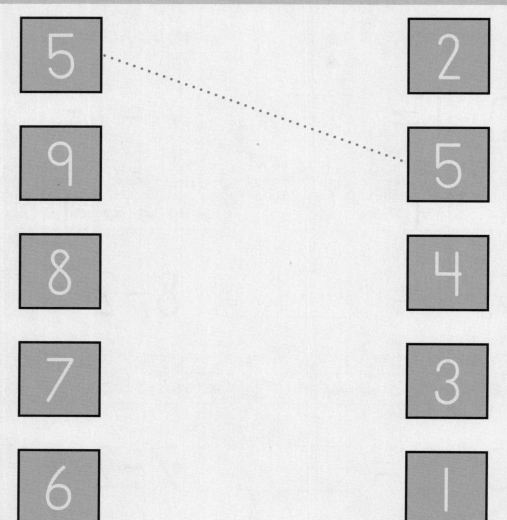

Count by 2s to continue the pattern.

Lesson 9.1B

7 - 1		8 - 0
	6	
9 - 0		6 - 0
	7	
7 - 0		8 - 1
	8	
9 - 1		9 - 2
	9	
8 - 2		10 - 1

Complete.

$5 - 0 =$ _____ $5 - 5 =$ _____

$6 - 0 =$ _____ $6 - 6 =$ _____

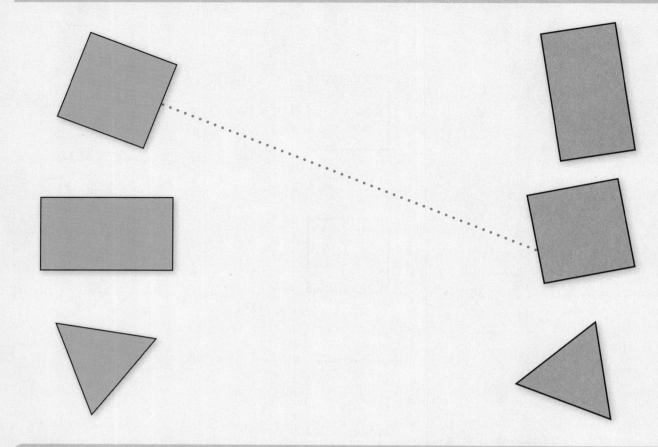

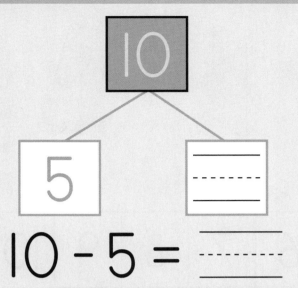

$$10 - 5 = \underline{}$$

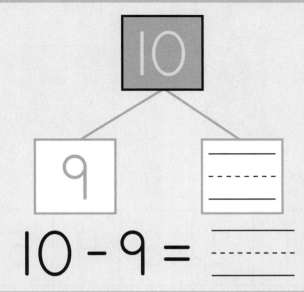

$$10 - 9 = \underline{}$$

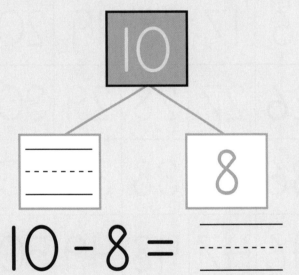

$$10 - 8 = \underline{}$$

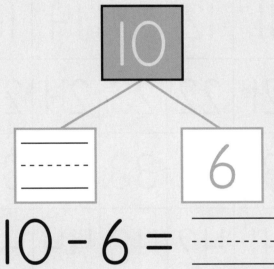

$$10 - 6 = \underline{}$$

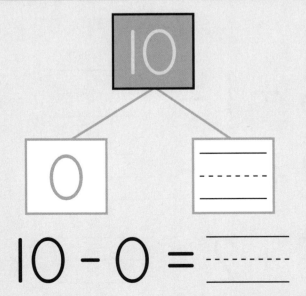

$$10 - 0 = \underline{}$$

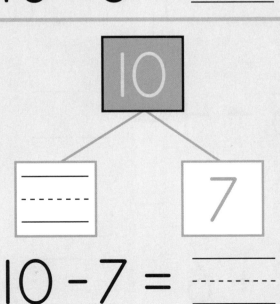

$$10 - 7 = \underline{}$$

Draw a line of symmetry for each shape.

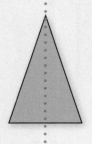  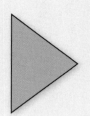 

Color the numbers you say when you count by 2s.

1	2	3	4	5	6	7	8	9	10
11	12	13	14	15	16	17	18	19	20
21	22	23	24	25	26	27	28	29	30
31	32	33	34	35	36	37	38	39	40
41	42	43	44	45	46	47	48	49	50

Complete.

$5 + 4 =$ _____ $8 + 1 =$ _____

$3 + 3 =$ _____ $2 + 7 =$ _____

$3 + 6 =$ _____ $5 + 2 =$ _____

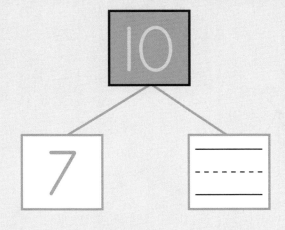

$$7 + \text{\_\_\_\_} = 10$$

$$10 - 7 = \text{\_\_\_\_}$$

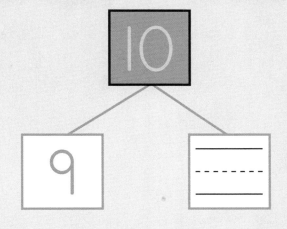

$$9 + \text{\_\_\_\_} = 10$$

$$10 - 9 = \text{\_\_\_\_}$$

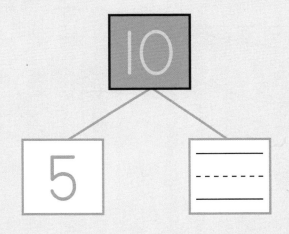

$$5 + \text{\_\_\_\_} = 10$$

$$10 - 5 = \text{\_\_\_\_}$$

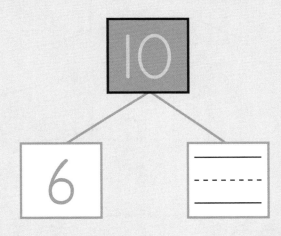

$$6 + \text{\_\_\_\_} = 10$$

$$10 - 6 = \text{\_\_\_\_}$$

Color the triangles red.
Color the rectangles green.
Color the circles blue.

Copy the shape.

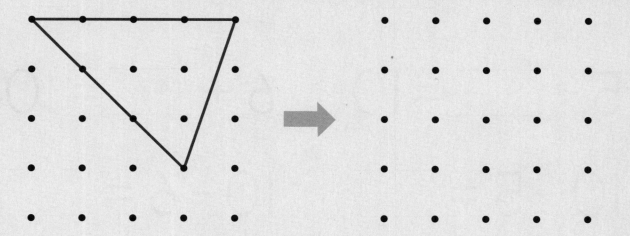

Lesson 9.4B

Tic-Tac-Toe
Game Board

4	3	5
6	5	6
7	4	3

$$9 - 4 = \text{\_\_\_\_\_}$$

$$6 - 4 = \text{\_\_\_\_\_}$$

$$7 - 3 = \text{\_\_\_\_\_}$$

$$8 - 4 = \text{\_\_\_\_\_}$$

$$10 - 3 = \text{\_\_\_\_\_}$$

$$7 - 4 = \text{\_\_\_\_\_}$$

$$8 - 3 = \text{\_\_\_\_\_}$$

$$9 - 3 = \text{\_\_\_\_\_}$$

$$6 - 3 = \text{\_\_\_\_\_}$$

$$5 - 4 = \text{\_\_\_\_\_}$$

Complete.

7 – 3 = _____   10 – 5 = _____

8 – 8 = _____   6 – 4 = _____

9 – 4 = _____   7 – 2 = _____

Color the addition facts that equal the number in the star.

5	6	7
7 – 2	10 – 4	9 – 3
9 – 4	7 – 1	8 – 4
6 – 1	8 – 3	10 – 3
8 – 3	6 – 0	8 – 1
10 – 3	9 – 3	9 – 2

Color the rectangles. X the shapes that are not rectangles.

Complete.

Lesson 10.2B

Complete the fact families to match.

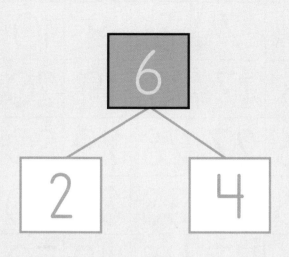

$$2 + 4 = \text{-------}$$

$$4 + 2 = \text{-------}$$

$$6 - 4 = \text{-------}$$

$$6 - 2 = \text{-------}$$

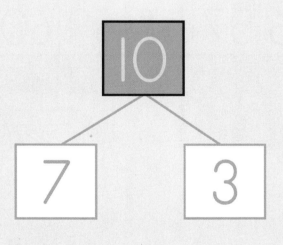

$$7 + \text{-------} = 10$$

$$\text{-------} + \text{-------} = 10$$

$$10 - 7 = \text{-------}$$

$$10 - \text{-------} = \text{-------}$$

Complete.

$$9 - 2 = \text{-------}$$

$$7 - 4 = \text{-------}$$

$$8 - 3 = \text{-------}$$

$$9 - 3 = \text{-------}$$

$$10 - 2 = \text{-------}$$

$$8 - 4 = \text{-------}$$

1	2	3	4	5	6	7	8	9	10
11	12	13	14	15	16	17	18	19	20
21	22	23	24	25	26	27	28	29	30
31	32	33	34	35	36	37	38	39	40
41	42	43	44	45	46	47	48	49	50
51	52	53	54	55	56	57	58	59	60

Fill the outline with pattern blocks. Write how many blocks you use.

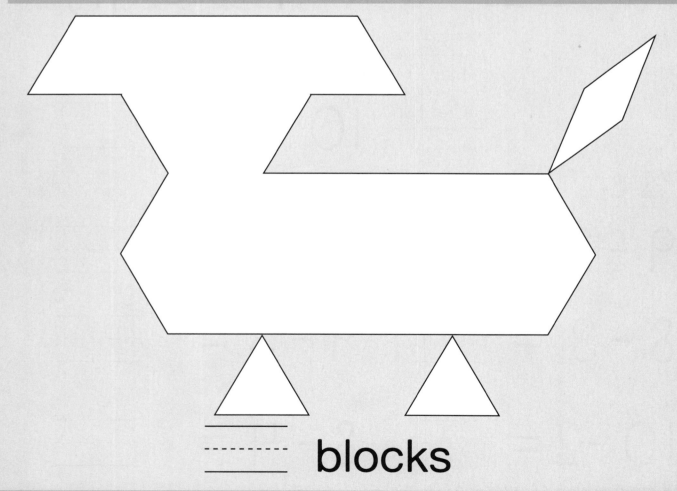

_____
------- blocks

Complete the fact family to match,

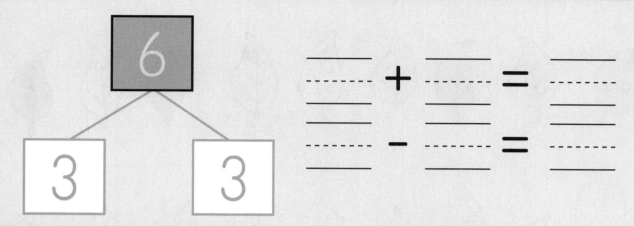

Complete. Then match the facts that are in the same fact family.

8 - 3 =

10 - 3 =

9 - 4 =

8 - 4 =

7 - 3 =

7 + 3 =

5 + 4 =

4 + 4 =

5 + 3 =

4 + 3 =

Color the leaves to complete the patterns.

X the shape that is different from the rest.

Subtraction Climb to the Top
Game Boards

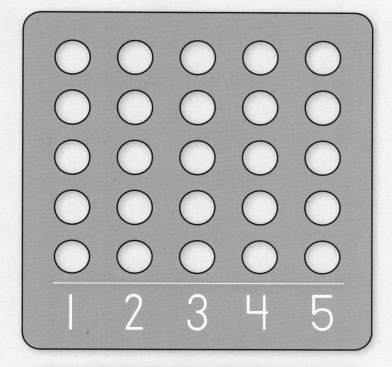

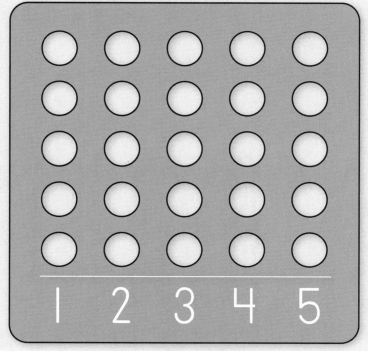

9 – 7 = _____   8 – 5 = _____

8 – 6 = _____   10 – 8 = _____

10 – 9 = _____   9 – 6 = _____

8 – 7 = _____   9 – 8 = _____

9 – 5 = _____   7 – 6 = _____

Draw a line that splits each cake in half.

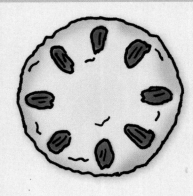

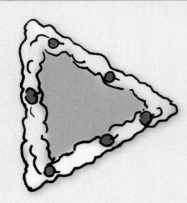

7 - 6		8 - 7
9 - 7		6 - 5
7 - 5	**0**	8 - 8
9 - 8	**1**	7 - 7
6 - 5		10 - 8
9 - 9	**2**	6 - 6
8 - 6		10 - 9

Write the number that comes before and after.

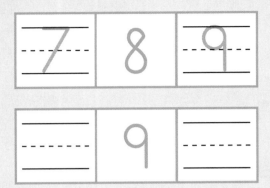

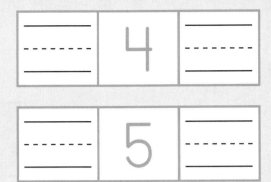

Complete the fact family to match the Part-Total Diagram.

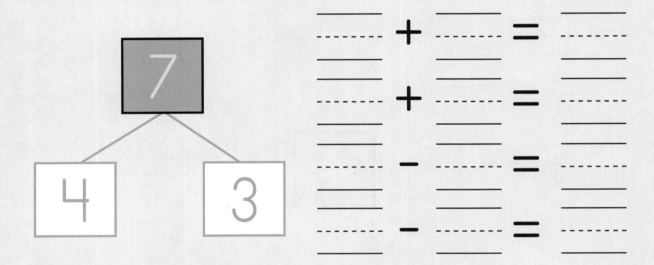

Draw lines that split each cake into fourths.

Complete.

10 - 5 = ...

8 - 5 = ...

10 - 7 = ...

8 - 6 = ...

6 - 4 = ...

9 - 6 = ...

10 - 6 = ...

9 - 5 = ...

9 - 7 = ...

7 - 5 = ...

Use the key to color the mittens.

Key
9 - blue
10 - purple

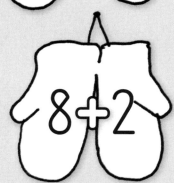

1	2	3	4	5	6	7	8	9	10
11	12	13	14	15	16	17	18	19	20
21	22	23	24	25	26	27	28	29	30
31	32	33	34	35	36	37	38	39	40
41	42	43	44	45	46	47	48	49	50
51	52	53	54	55	56	57	58	59	60

Match.

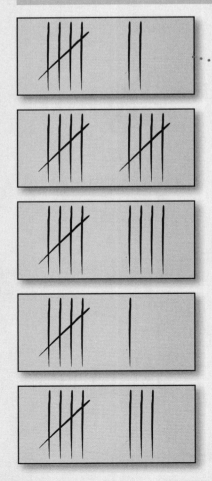

6

7

8

9

10

Complete.

9 − 8 = _____   10 − 8 = _____

10 − 9 = _____   7 − 6 = _____

8 − 7 = _____   6 − 4 = _____

9 − 5 = _____   8 − 4 = _____

7 − 5 = _____   8 − 5 = _____

Complete the fact family to match the Part-Total Diagram.

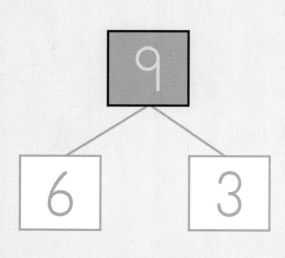

_____ + _____ = _____

_____ + _____ = _____

_____ − _____ = _____

_____ − _____ = _____

Complete.

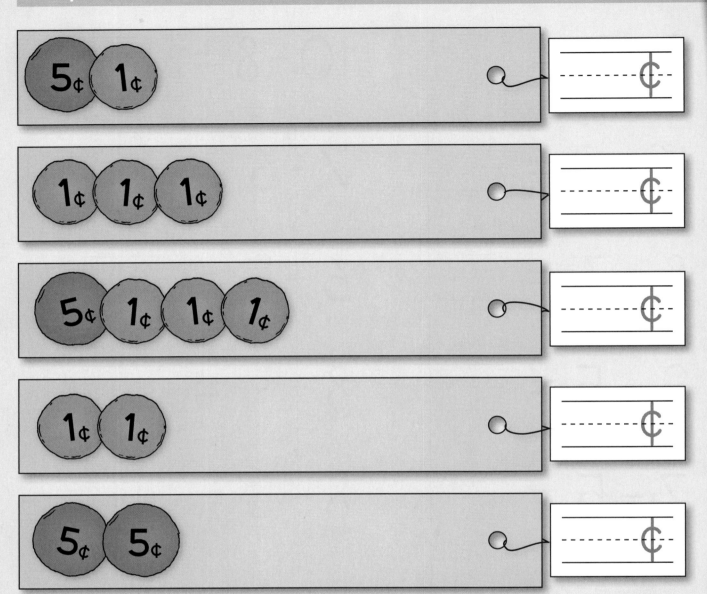

Copy the shape.

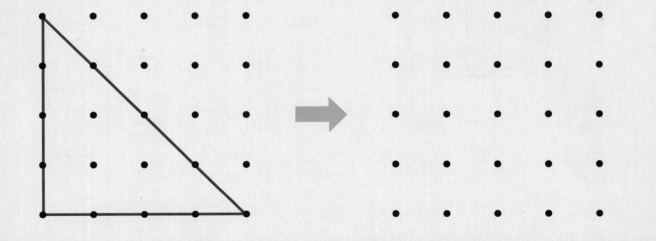

Trace the numbers.

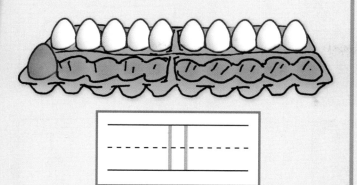

11

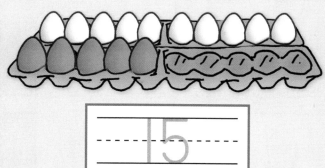

15

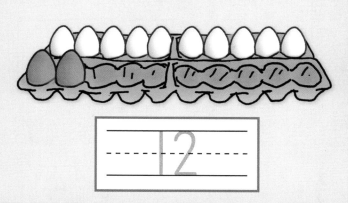

12

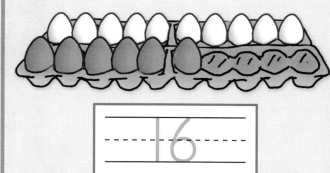

16

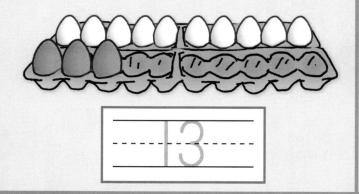

13

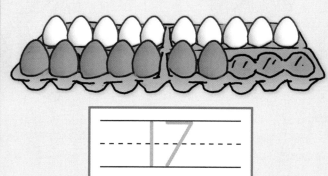

17

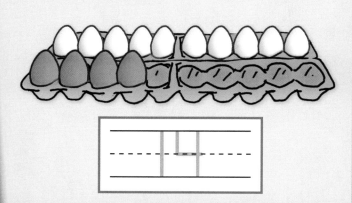

14

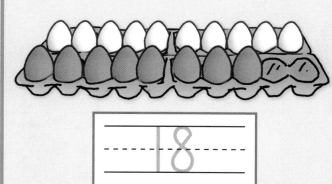

18

Match.

9 − 5

10 − 6

8 − 5

2

3

4

10 − 8

6 − 4

9 − 6

Draw a line of symmetry for each item.

Count by 2s to continue the pattern.

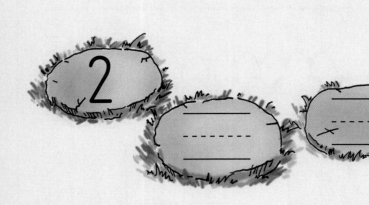

2

2

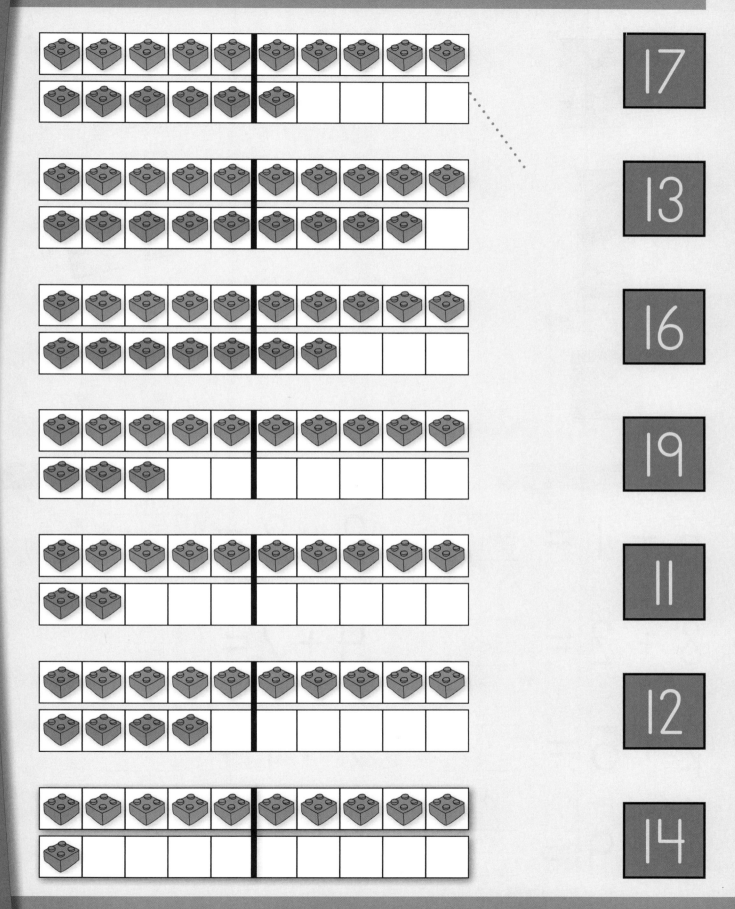

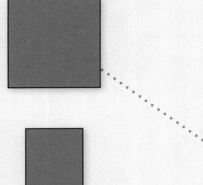

Complete.

6 + 1 = _____   2 + 3 = _____

8 + 2 = _____   4 + 2 = _____

2 + 5 = _____   7 + 1 = _____

0 + 9 = _____   1 + 5 = _____

16

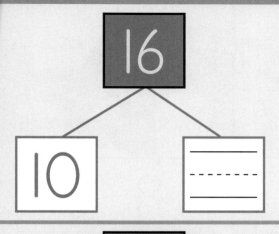

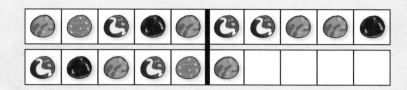

$10 +$ _____ $= 16$

18

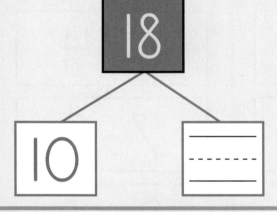

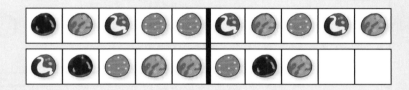

$10 +$ _____ $= 18$

_____

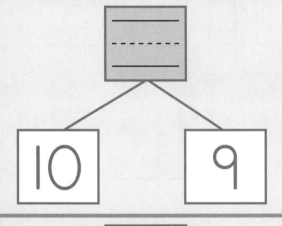

10   9

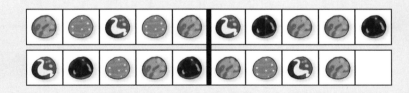

$10 + 9 =$ _____

_____

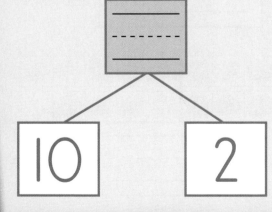

10   2

$10 + 2 =$ _____

Color the subtraction facts that equal the number in the star.

⭐ 2	⭐ 1	⭐ 4
9 – 7	5 – 4	9 – 3
8 – 4	10 – 9	8 – 4
7 – 5	9 – 8	7 – 3
8 – 6	9 – 7	9 – 5

Write how many.

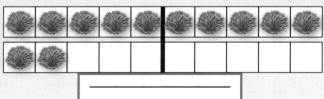

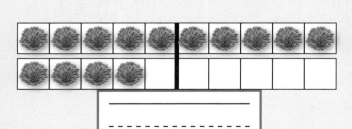

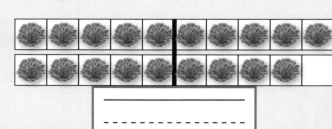

12¢

14¢

13¢

Complete.

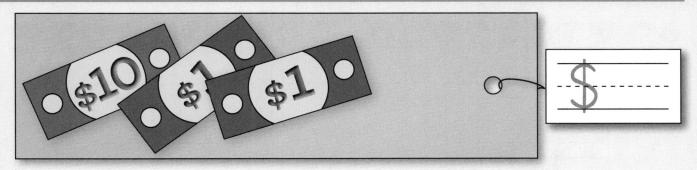

$

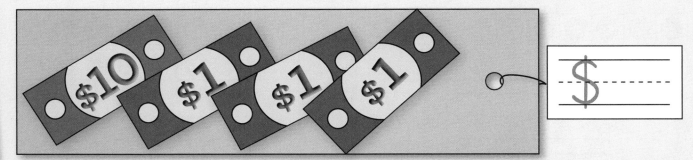

$

4 + 5 = _____

6 + 4 = _____

3 + 3 = _____

3 + 5 = _____

6 + 3 = _____

4 + 4 = _____

5 + 5 = _____

3 + 7 = _____

Write how many.

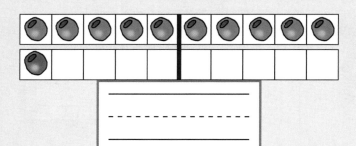

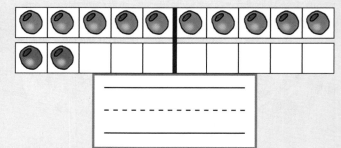

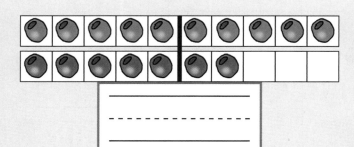

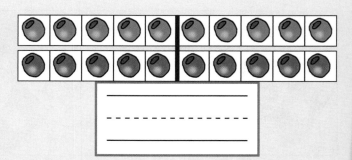

Circle the greater number in each pair.

16

14

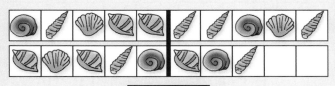

18

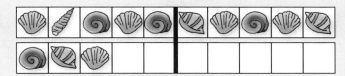

13

12   10

20   19

17   15

16   11

Complete.

14

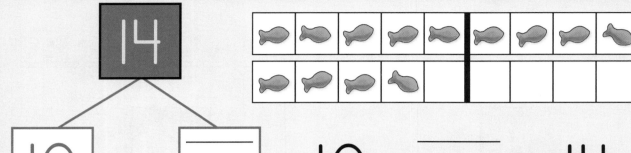

10   _____

$10 + \underline{\hspace{2cm}} = 14$

17

10   _____

$10 + \underline{\hspace{2cm}} = 17$

Complete.

$4 + 1 = \underline{\hspace{2cm}}$ $0 + 7 = \underline{\hspace{2cm}}$

$6 + 2 = \underline{\hspace{2cm}}$ $5 + 3 = \underline{\hspace{2cm}}$

$5 + 4 = \underline{\hspace{2cm}}$ $3 + 2 = \underline{\hspace{2cm}}$

$9 + 1 = \underline{\hspace{2cm}}$ $5 + 1 = \underline{\hspace{2cm}}$

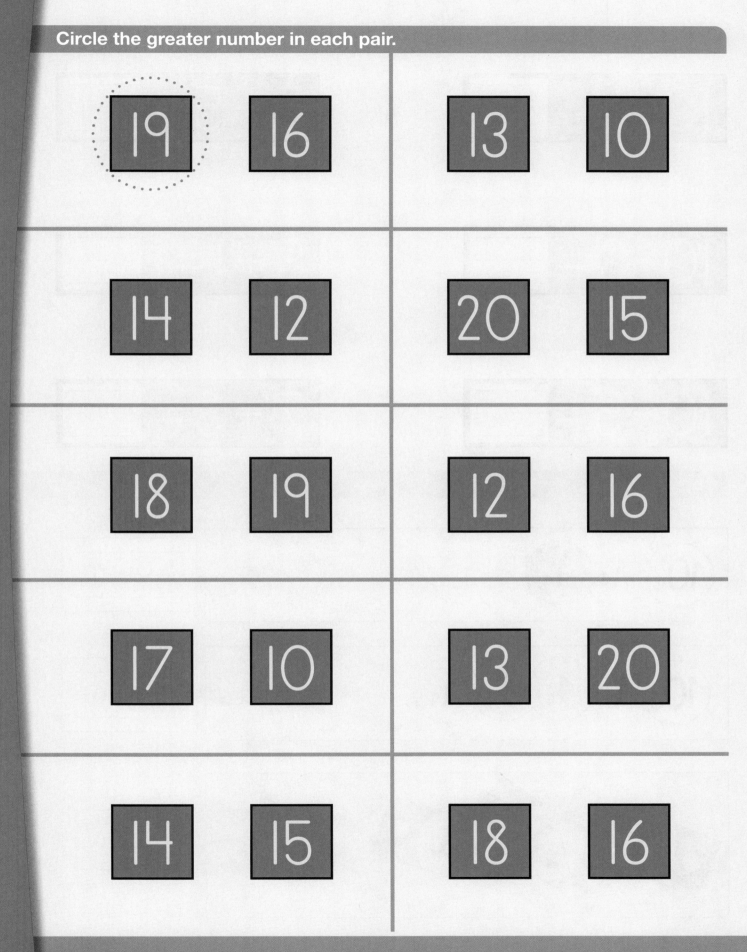

Complete. Then match the facts that are in the same fact family.

$$10 - 1 = \boxed{}$$

$$5 + 5 = \boxed{}$$

$$10 - 3 = \boxed{}$$

$$9 + 1 = \boxed{}$$

$$10 - 5 = \boxed{}$$

$$7 + 3 = \boxed{}$$

Complete.

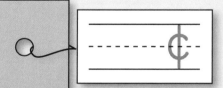

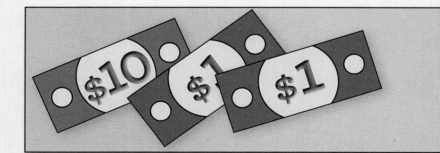

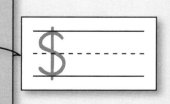

Even Numbers to 20

1	2	3	4	5	6	7	8	9	10
11	12	13	14	15	16	17	18	19	20

Color the odd numbers on the 100 Chart.

Odd Numbers to 20

1	2	3	4	5	6	7	8	9	10
11	12	13	14	15	16	17	18	19	20

Circle the greater number in each pair.

 19   16   13   10

14   12   20   15

18   19   12   16

Match.

8 + 1   8   2 + 6

4 + 4   8 + 0

2 + 7   9   5 + 4

3 + 6   5 + 3

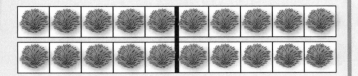

18 + _2_ = 20

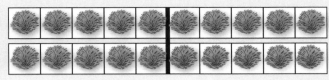

15 + ____ = 20

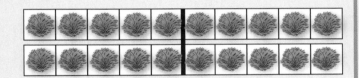

14 + ____ = 20

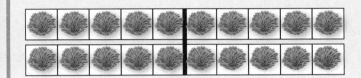

19 + ____ = 20

11 + ____ = 20

17 + ____ = 20

12 + ____ = 20

10 + ____ = 20

Complete.

9 − 1 = _____   10 − 4 = _____

7 − 4 = _____   6 − 5 = _____

5 − 0 = _____   8 − 3 = _____

Color the odd numbers on the 100 Chart.

Odd Numbers to 20

1	2	3	4	5	6	7	8	9	10
11	12	13	14	15	16	17	18	19	20

Draw a congruent shape.

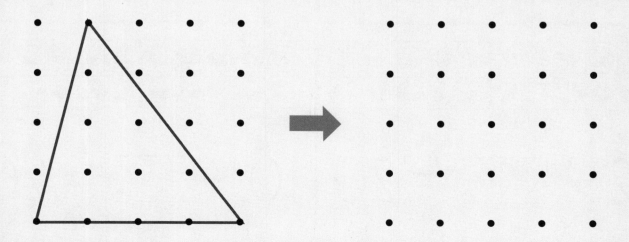

Heads and Tails Tally Chart

Heads

Tails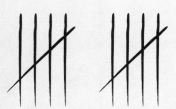

How many heads?

_____
- - - - - - - -
_____

How many tails?

_____
- - - - - - - -
_____

Are there more
heads or more tails?

_____
- - - - - - - - - - - - - - - - - -
_____

How many more?

_____
- - - - - -

How many coin flips
in all are in the chart?

_____
- - - - - - - -
_____

$10 - 8 =$ _____ $9 - 7 =$ _____

$9 - 3 =$ _____ $4 - 0 =$ _____

$8 - 2 =$ _____ $7 - 4 =$ _____

$8 - 6 =$ _____ $9 - 5 =$ _____

Match.

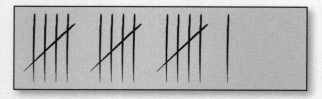
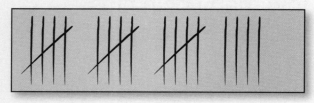
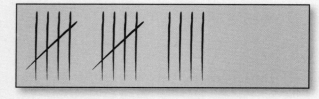
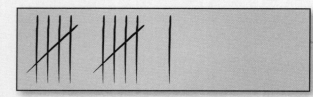

Number Race Bar Graph

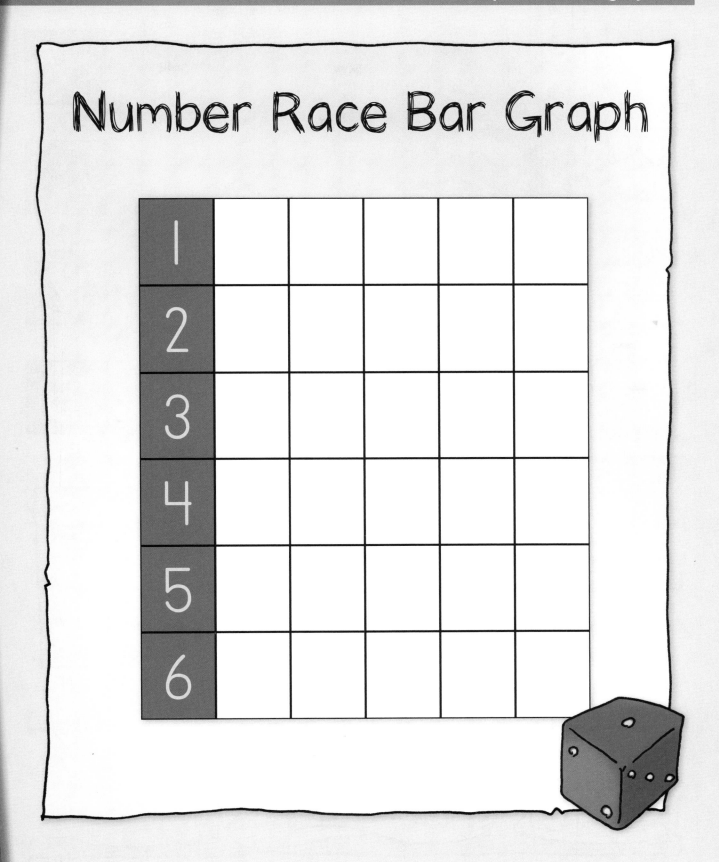

Match.

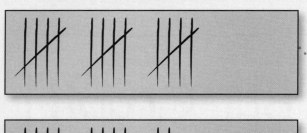

17

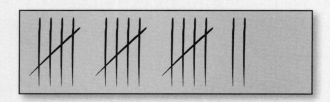

20

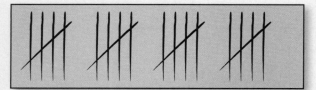

12

15

Use the key to color the hats.

Key
0 - blue
1 - red
2 - green

6-5

7-6

10-8

9-8

8-6

6-6

7-5

9-7

Children by Family

Lees | Petersons | Smiths | Garcias

How many children
do the Lees have?

_____

Which family has
the **most** children?

_____

Which family has the
least number of children?

_____

How many children
are in all 4 families?

_____

Complete.

$$10 + \underline{} = 18$$

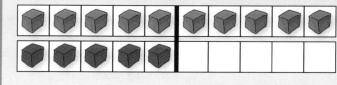

$$10 + \underline{} = 15$$

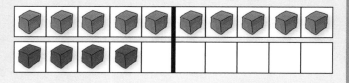

$$10 + \underline{} = 14$$

$$10 + \underline{} = 19$$

Color the addition facts that equal the number in the star.

8

6 + 2
4 + 4
3 + 5
2 + 7

9

5 + 3
4 + 5
6 + 3
8 + 1

10

5 + 5
7 + 3
8 + 3
8 + 2

Girls and Boys

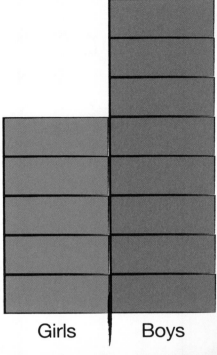

Girls   Boys

How many girls?

_____
- - - - - - - -
_____

How many boys?

_____
- - - - - - - -
_____

Are there more
girls or more boys?

_____
- - - - - - - - - - - - - - - -
_____

How many more?

_____
- - - - - - - -
_____

How many children
in all are on the chart?

_____
- - - - - - - -
_____

Lesson 14.4A

111

6 - 5 = ...

7 - 2 = ...

7 - 6 = ...

9 - 8 = ...

10 - 9 = ...

8 - 7 = ...

6 - 6 = ...

10 - 8 = ...

Complete.

11 + ... = 20

17 + ... = 20

12 + ... = 20

16 + ... = 20

Match. Each bag has 10 cookies.

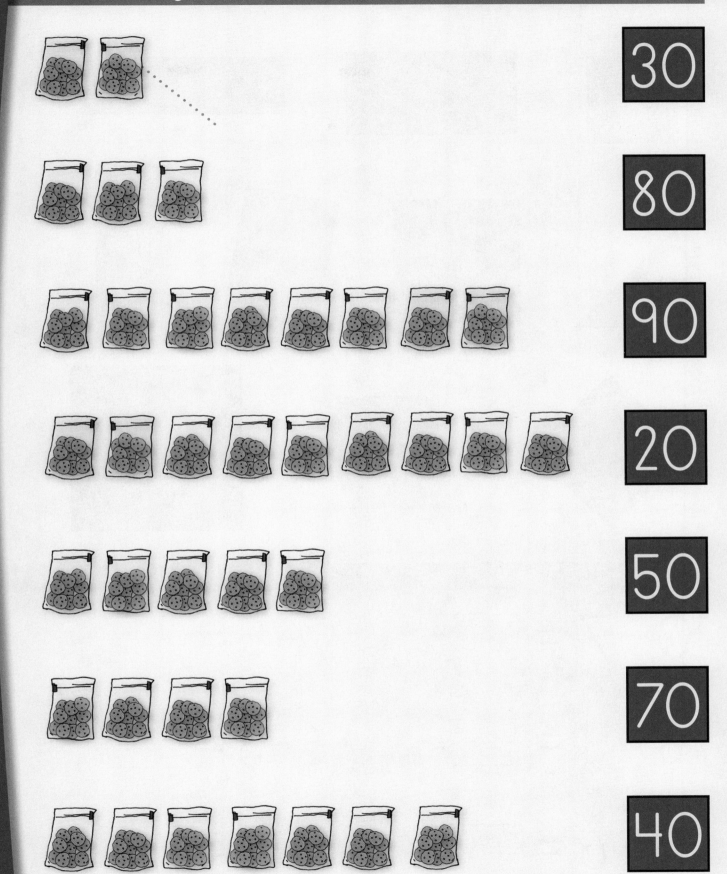

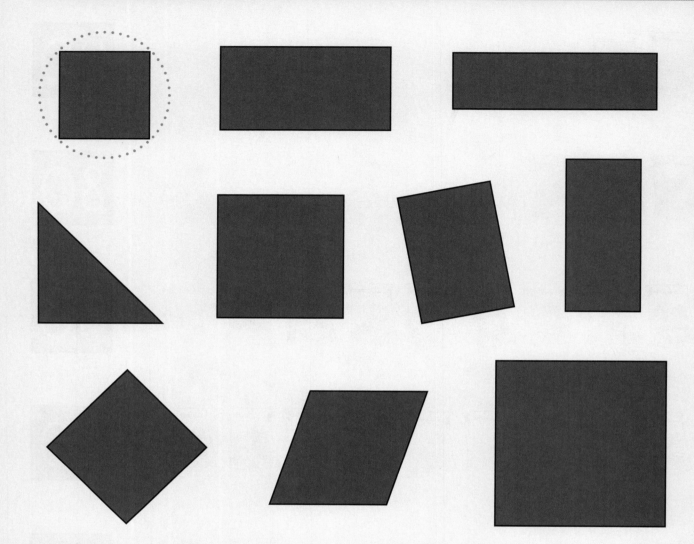

Complete.

$$10 - 7 = \text{\underline{\hspace{2cm}}}$$

$$7 - 5 = \text{\underline{\hspace{2cm}}}$$

$$8 - 4 = \text{\underline{\hspace{2cm}}}$$

$$6 - 3 = \text{\underline{\hspace{2cm}}}$$

$$9 - 6 = \text{\underline{\hspace{2cm}}}$$

$$9 - 2 = \text{\underline{\hspace{2cm}}}$$

Complete.

30 + 10 = _____   20 + 20 = _____

40 + 20 = _____   10 + 20 = _____

 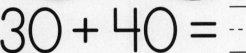  

30 + 40 = _____   50 + 10 = _____

20 + 30 = _____   20 + 40 = _____

9 + 1 = _____   5 + 1 = _____

4 + 5 = _____   2 + 6 = _____

8 + 0 = _____   3 + 7 = _____

Match pairs that make 20.

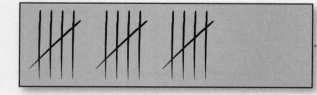

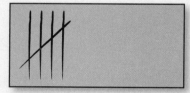

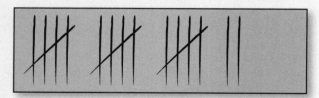
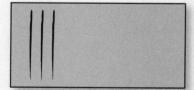

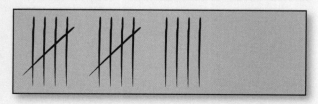
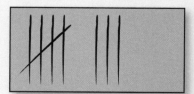

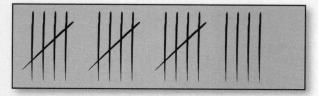
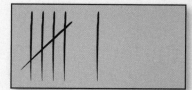

$$50 - 10 = \text{-------}$$

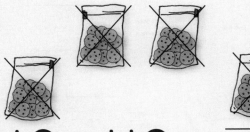

$$40 - 40 = \text{-------}$$

$$60 - 20 = \text{-------}$$

$$60 - 50 = \text{-------}$$

$$30 - 10 = \text{-------}$$

$$50 - 20 = \text{-------}$$

$$40 - 30 = \text{-------}$$

$$50 - 10 = \text{-------}$$

$$9 - 5 = \underline{\hspace{2cm}}$$

$$10 - 5 = \underline{\hspace{2cm}}$$

$$8 - 2 = \underline{\hspace{2cm}}$$

$$6 - 5 = \underline{\hspace{2cm}}$$

$$10 - 1 = \underline{\hspace{2cm}}$$

$$9 - 9 = \underline{\hspace{2cm}}$$

Write how many.

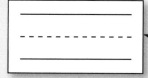

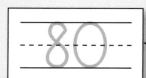

Complete.

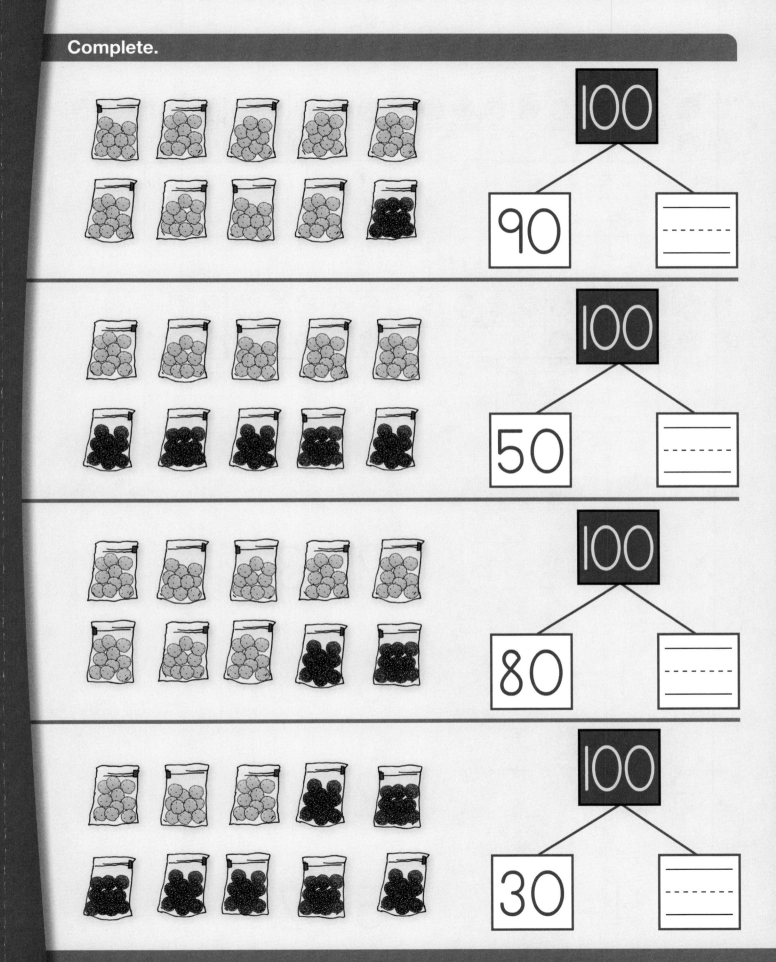

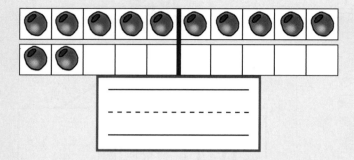

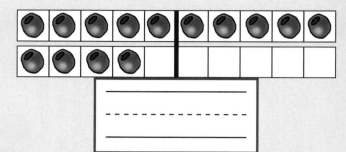

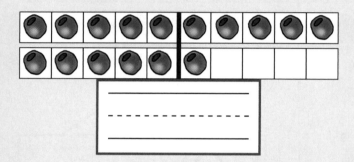

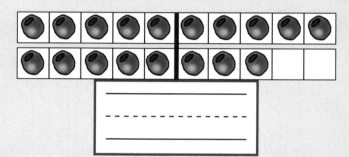

Complete.

$$8 + 2 = \underline{\quad\quad}$$

$$2 + 3 = \underline{\quad\quad}$$

$$4 + 1 = \underline{\quad\quad}$$

$$6 + 3 = \underline{\quad\quad}$$

$$7 + 0 = \underline{\quad\quad}$$

$$2 + 2 = \underline{\quad\quad}$$

$$4 + 4 = \underline{\quad\quad}$$

$$5 + 2 = \underline{\quad\quad}$$

Complete.

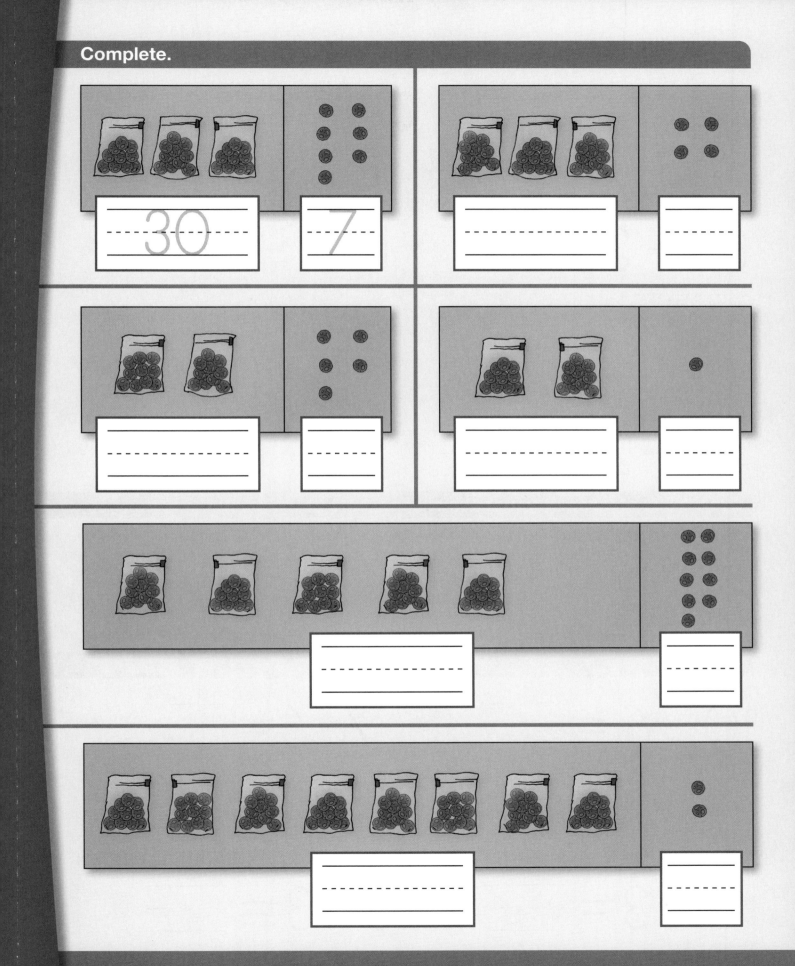

$30 + 30 =$ _____

$10 + 40 =$ _____

$30 - 20 =$ _____

$50 - 10 =$ _____

Draw a line of symmetry for each shape.

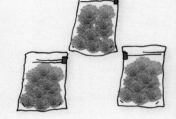

Complete.

$10 - 6 =$ _____ $7 - 6 =$ _____

$8 - 7 =$ _____ $6 - 4 =$ _____

$8 - 3 =$ _____ $10 - 3 =$ _____

Write how many.

tens	ones
4	5

tens	ones

tens	ones

tens	ones

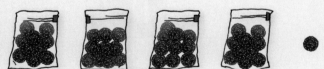

tens	ones

tens	ones

Complete.

7 + 3 = _____   5 + 3 = _____

4 + 3 = _____   2 + 4 = _____

6 + 1 = _____   3 + 6 = _____

Match pairs that make 100.

90	50
80	60
50	10
40	30
70	20

35

42

40

34

43

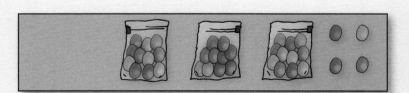

23

Complete.

$$10 - 8 = \text{_____}$$

$$9 - 7 = \text{_____}$$

$$9 - 3 = \text{_____}$$

$$4 - 0 = \text{_____}$$

$$8 - 8 = \text{_____}$$

$$7 - 4 = \text{_____}$$

Complete.

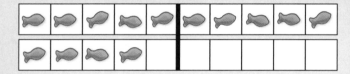

$$10 + 4 = \text{_____}$$

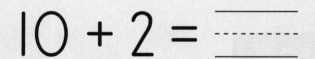

$$10 + 2 = \text{_____}$$

$$10 + 1 = \text{_____}$$

$$10 + 3 = \text{_____}$$

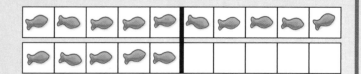

$$10 + 5 = \text{_____}$$

$$10 + 7 = \text{_____}$$

Complete.

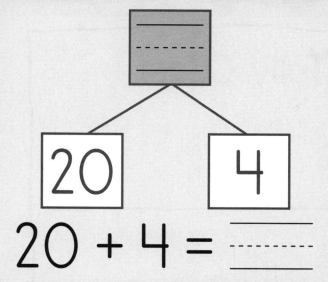

20 + 4 = _____

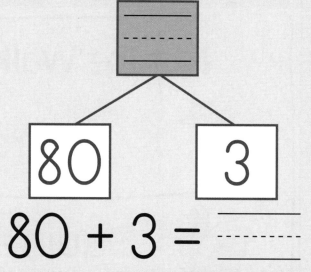

80 + 3 = _____

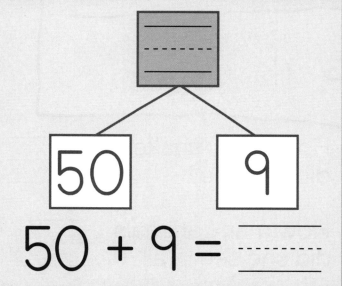

50 + 9 = _____

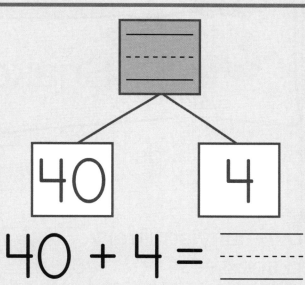

40 + 4 = _____

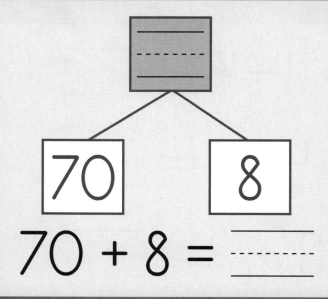

70 + 8 = _____

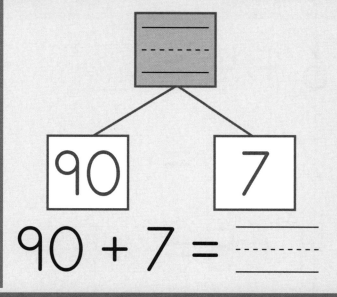

90 + 7 = _____

Sara made a tally chart of the animals she saw on a nature walk. Use the chart to answer the questions.

Nature Walk Tally Chart

🐦	Birds	|||| ||
🐿️	Squirrels	||||
🐛	Snakes		

How many birds did she see? _____

How many snakes did she see? _____

How many squirrels did she see? _____

How many animals did she see in all? _____

Complete.

$6 + 4 =$ _____ $1 + 6 =$ _____

$7 + 2 =$ _____ $4 + 2 =$ _____

$4 + 5 =$ _____ $3 + 3 =$ _____

Circle the greater number in each pair.

(**39**) 26   73 82

54 62   37 28

78 79   52 45

37 40   37 30

7 70   91 19

Lesson 17.1A

Complete.

$30+50 =$ _____ $20+40 =$ _____

$60+30 =$ _____ $40+40 =$ _____

$70+20 =$ _____ $10+80 =$ _____

Color the even numbers on the 100 Chart.

Even Numbers to 20

1	2	3	4	5	6	7	8	9	10
11	12	13	14	15	16	17	18	19	20

Color the odd numbers on the 100 Chart.

Odd Numbers to 20

1	2	3	4	5	6	7	8	9	10
11	12	13	14	15	16	17	18	19	20

31	32	33	34	35	36
41	42		44	45	46
51	52			55	56
61	62		64		
71	72		74	75	76
	82	83	84	85	
91	92		94	95	96

Match.

5 + 5 = _____

0 + 9 = _____

4 + 6 = _____

8 + 1 = _____

7 + 1 = _____

3 + 5 = _____

Circle the greater number in each pair.

| 57 | 68 | | 88 | 90 |

| 64 | 62 | | 37 | 40 |

| 81 | 82 | | 60 | 70 |

32 + 1 = ------

28 + 1 = ------

 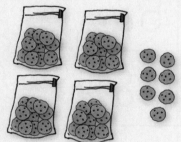

32 + 10 = ------

 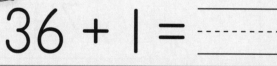

28 + 10 = ------

47 + 1 = ------

36 + 1 = ------

47 + 10 = ------

36 + 10 = ------

Complete.

$$10 - 4 = \underline{\quad\quad} \qquad 5 - 5 = \underline{\quad\quad}$$

$$9 - 1 = \underline{\quad\quad} \qquad 9 - 4 = \underline{\quad\quad}$$

$$8 - 5 = \underline{\quad\quad} \qquad 10 - 2 = \underline{\quad\quad}$$

Complete the missing numbers on the 100 Chart.

53	54	___	56	57	58
63	64	65	66	___	68
___	74	75	76	77	78
___	84	85	___	87	88
93	94	___	96	97	98

Complete the number patterns.

Pattern 1 (count by 10): 10, **20**, **30**, **40**, **50**, 60

Pattern 2 (count by 5): 5, **10**, 15, **20**, **25**, **30**

Pattern 3 (count by 1): **1**, **2**, **3**, 4, **5**, **6**

Pattern 4 (count by 10): 50, **60**, 70, **80**, **90**, 100

Pattern 5 (count by 5): 45, 50, **55**, **60**, **65**, 70

Pattern 6 (count by 1): 34, **35**, **36**, **37**, 38

Match pairs that make 100.

 10   50

40   60

30   80

50   90

20   70

Complete.

$10 + 0 =$ _____ $3 + 4 =$ _____

$2 + 7 =$ _____ $5 + 3 =$ _____

$1 + 8 =$ _____ $6 + 2 =$ _____

The map shows the animals' paths to the flowers.
Use the map to answer the questions.

How long is the
snail's ⬤ path? _____ inches

How long is the
ant's 🐜 path? _____ inches

How long is the
ladybug's 🐞 path? _____ inches

Which animal's path
is longest?

_____

_____

Which animal's path
is shortest?

_____

_____

9 + 1 = _____   5 + 1 = _____

4 + 5 = _____   2 + 6 = _____

8 + 0 = _____   3 + 7 = _____

Complete the missing numbers on the 100 chart.

	36	37	38	39	40
45	46	47		49	
55	56			59	60
	66	67	68	69	70
75	76	77	78	79	
85		87	88	89	90

Write the length of each ribbon.

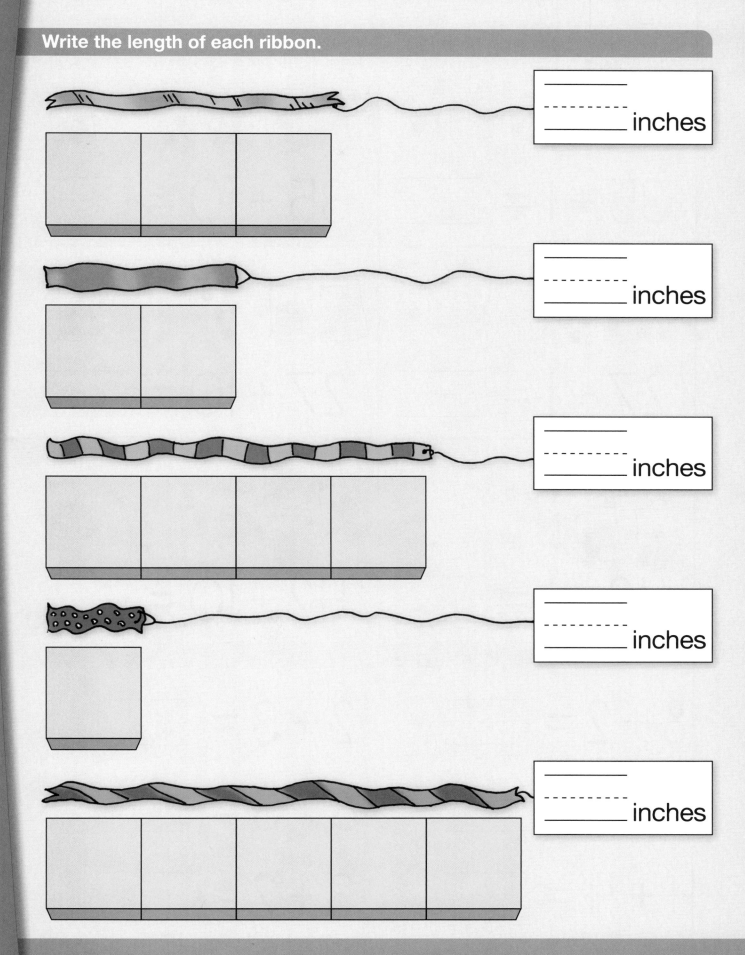

_____
- - - - - - - - - -
_____ inches

_____
- - - - - - - - - -
_____ inches

_____
- - - - - - - - - -
_____ inches

_____
- - - - - - - - - -
_____ inches

_____
- - - - - - - - - -
_____ inches

$35 + 1 =$ _____ $35 + 10 =$ _____

$27 + 1 =$ _____ $27 + 10 =$ _____

$42 + 1 =$ _____ $42 + 10 =$ _____

Complete.

$8 + 2 =$ _____ $2 + 3 =$ _____

$4 + 1 =$ _____ $6 + 3 =$ _____

$4 + 4 =$ _____ $3 + 2 =$ _____

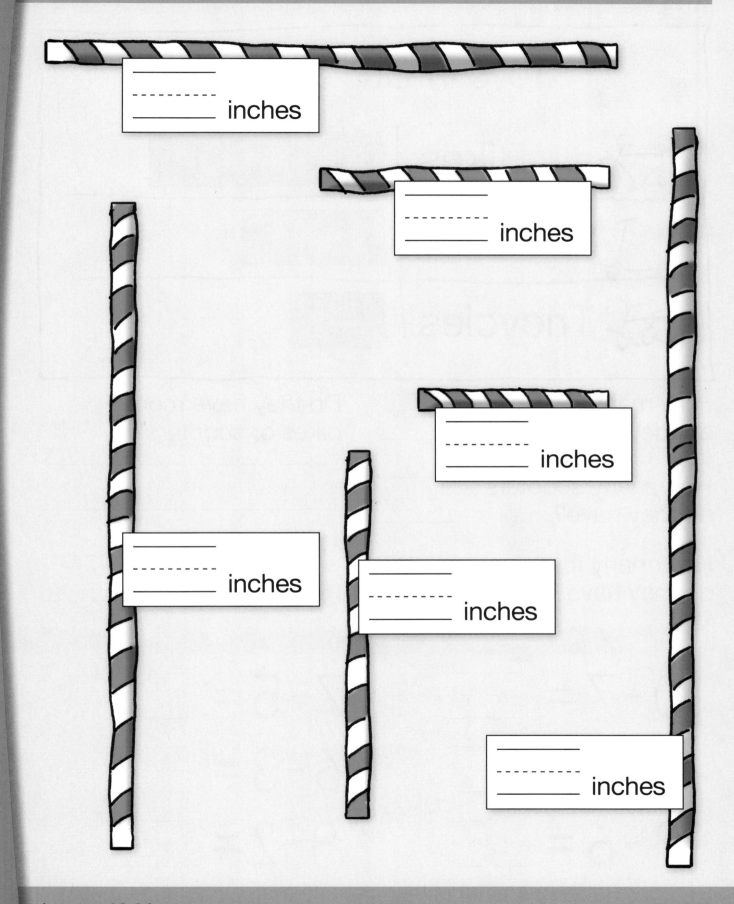

_____
- - - - - - - - -
_____ inches

_____
- - - - - - - - -
_____ inches

_____
- - - - - - - - -
_____ inches

_____
- - - - - - - - -
_____ inches

_____
- - - - - - - - -
_____ inches

_____
- - - - - - - - -
_____ inches

Michael made a bar graph of the toys in his family's garage. Use the bar graph to answer the questions.

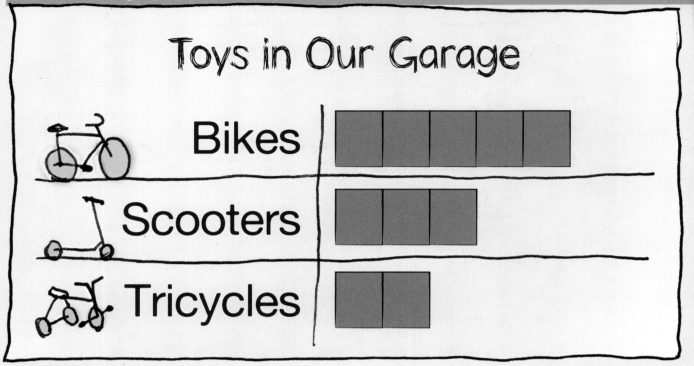

Toys in Our Garage

Bikes

Scooters

Tricycles

How many bikes do they have? _____

How many scooters do they have? _____

How many tricycles do they have? _____

Do they have more bikes or scooters?

_____

_____

How many more? _____

Complete.

$10 - 7 =$ _____

$8 - 4 =$ _____

$9 - 6 =$ _____

$7 - 5 =$ _____

$6 - 3 =$ _____

$9 - 2 =$ _____

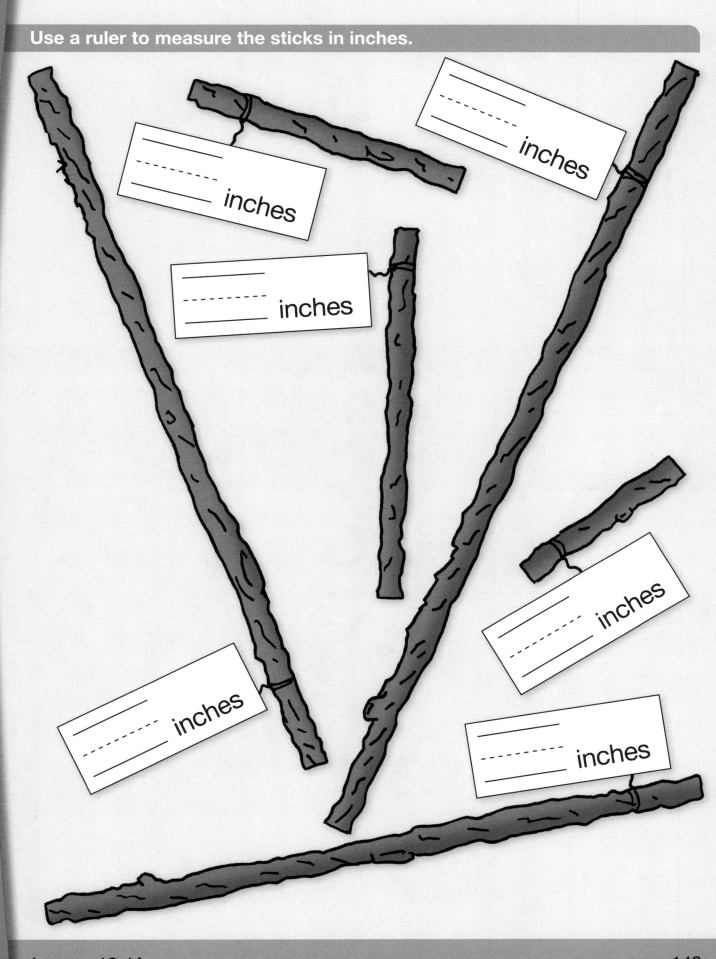

_____ inches

_____ inches

_____ inches

_____ inches

_____ inches

_____ inches

_____ inches

7 + 3 = _____   5 + 3 = _____

4 + 3 = _____   2 + 4 = _____

6 + 1 = _____   3 + 6 = _____

Write how many.

_____

_____

_____

_____

_____

Use a 1-foot ruler to see whether each object is shorter than a foot, about equal to a foot, or longer than a foot. Check the box that matches.

Object	Shorter than a foot	About equal to a foot	Longer than a foot
The length of this page		✓	
The width of this page			
Your hand			
Your foot			
Your bed			
Your pencil			
Your chair			

50 + 30 = _____

30 + 40 = _____

60 + 30 = _____

20 + 70 = _____

80 - 20 = _____

60 - 10 = _____

70 - 30 = _____

90 - 30 = _____

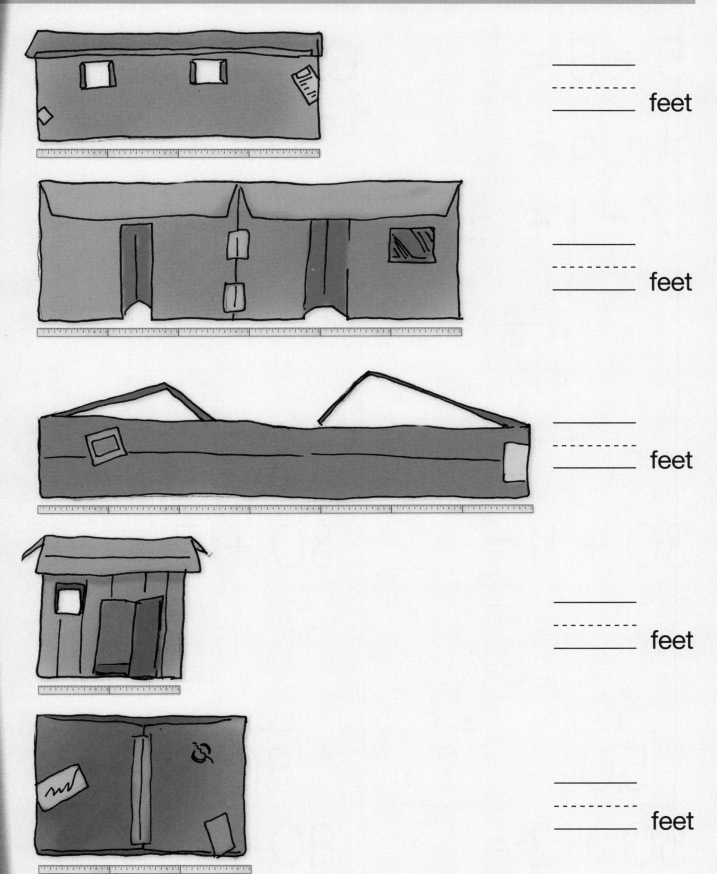

_____
- - - - - - - - - -
_____ feet

_____
- - - - - - - - - -
_____ feet

_____
- - - - - - - - - -
_____ feet

_____
- - - - - - - - - -
_____ feet

_____
- - - - - - - - - -
_____ feet

5 + 5 = _____   0 + 9 = _____

4 + 6 = _____   8 + 1 = _____

7 + 1 = _____   3 + 5 = _____

Complete.

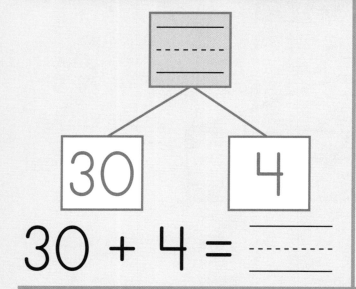

30 + 4 = _____

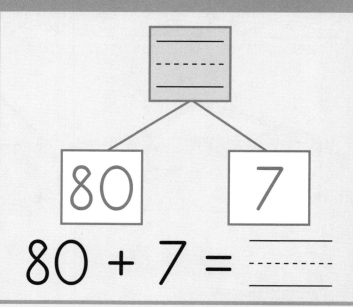

80 + 7 = _____

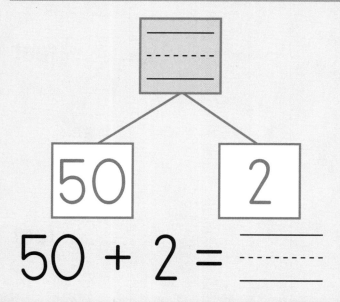

50 + 2 = _____

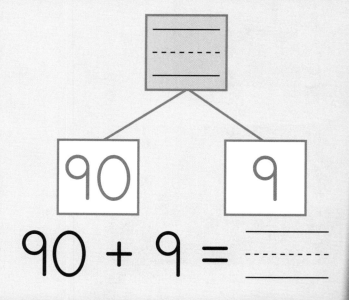

90 + 9 = _____

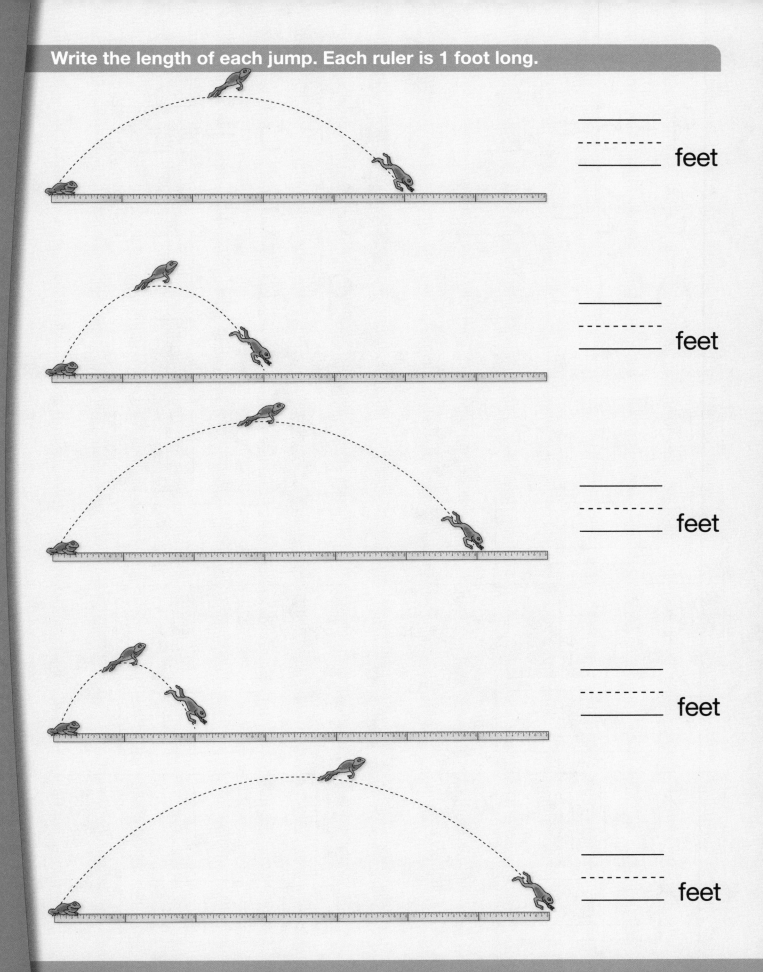

_____
- - - - - - _____ feet
_____

_____
- - - - - - _____ feet
_____

_____
- - - - - - _____ feet
_____

_____
- - - - - - _____ feet
_____

_____
- - - - - - _____ feet
_____

$$9 - 5 = \rule{3cm}{0.4pt}$$ $$10 - 5 = \rule{3cm}{0.4pt}$$

$$8 - 2 = \rule{3cm}{0.4pt}$$ $$6 - 5 = \rule{3cm}{0.4pt}$$

$$10 - 1 = \rule{3cm}{0.4pt}$$ $$9 - 9 = \rule{3cm}{0.4pt}$$

Write how many.

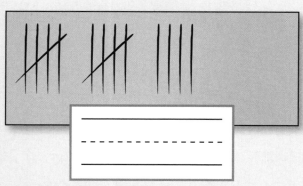

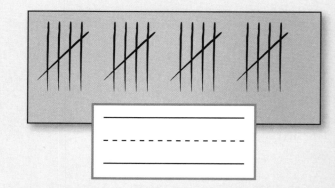

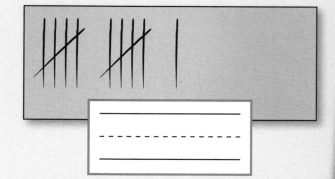

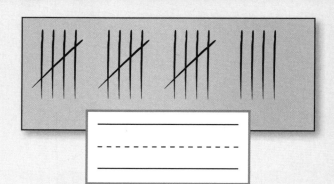

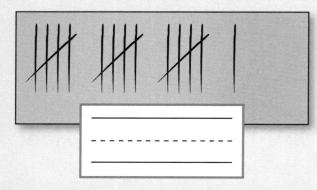

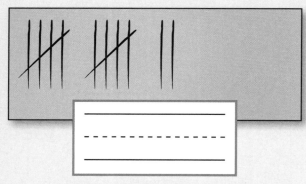

Write the height of each robot. Each ruler is 1 foot long.

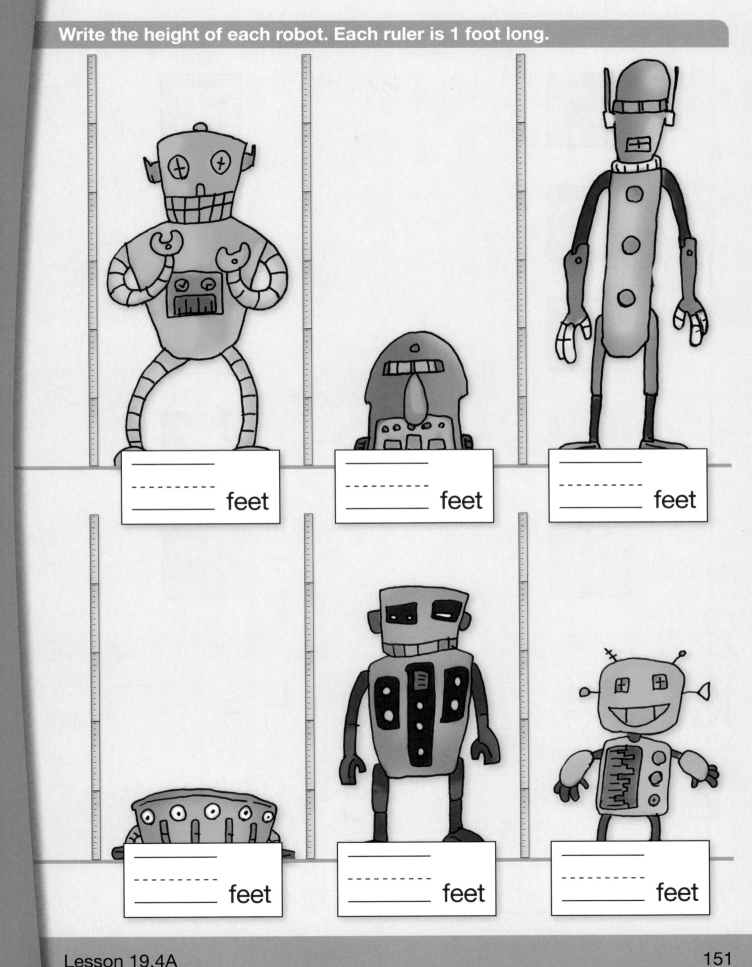

_____ feet

_____ feet

_____ feet

_____ feet

_____ feet

_____ feet

20   50

50   60

30   80

40   90

10   70

Complete.

$$10 + 0 = \rule{2cm}{0.4pt}$$

$$3 + 4 = \rule{2cm}{0.4pt}$$

$$2 + 7 = \rule{2cm}{0.4pt}$$

$$5 + 3 = \rule{2cm}{0.4pt}$$

$$1 + 8 = \rule{2cm}{0.4pt}$$

$$6 + 2 = \rule{2cm}{0.4pt}$$

See *Instructor Guide* for directions on how to play.
Save these game boards for future lessons.

153

Adding 9s Bingo
Game Boards

B	I	N	G	O
13	14	17	16	12
16	11	15	12	17
18	15	FREE	11	10
11	18	12	14	13
14	10	13	17	15

B	I	N	G	O
10	13	11	16	17
15	11	16	10	14
13	14	FREE	12	15
17	18	13	14	12
16	12	15	13	18

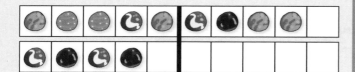

$$9 + 4 = \underline{\quad\quad}$$

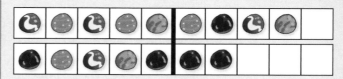

$$9 + 7 = \underline{\quad\quad}$$

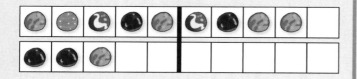

$$9 + 2 = \underline{\quad\quad}$$

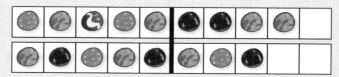

$$9 + 6 = \underline{\quad\quad}$$

$$9 + 3 = \underline{\quad\quad}$$

$$9 + 8 = \underline{\quad\quad}$$

$$9 + 5 = \underline{\quad\quad}$$

$$9 + 9 = \underline{\quad\quad}$$

Complete.

9 + 5 = _____   9 + 3 = _____

9 + 8 = _____   9 + 4 = _____

9 + 7 = _____   9 + 2 = _____

9 + 6 = _____   9 + 9 = _____

Use the key to color the flowers.

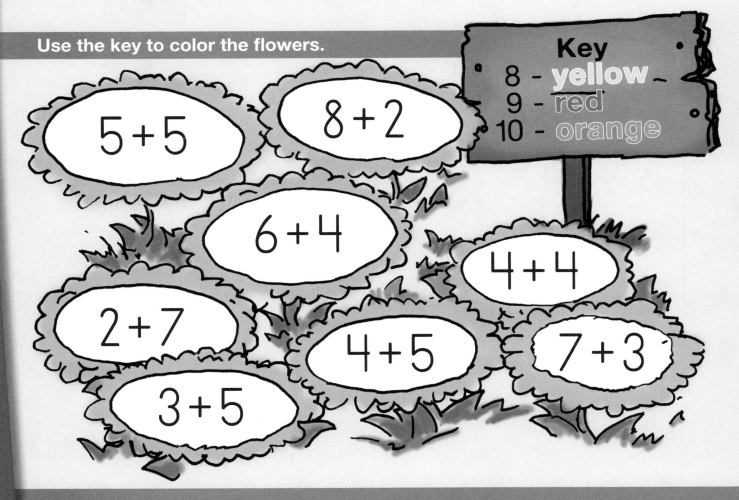

Key
8 - yellow
9 - red
10 - orange

5+5   8+2   6+4   2+7   4+4   4+5   7+3   3+5

50 + 5	81
60 + 3	63
30 + 6	55
80 + 1	18
10 + 8	36

Color the circles. X the shapes that are not circles.

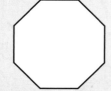
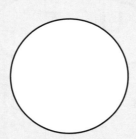
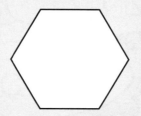

9 + 4	11	5 + 9
9 + 7	12	4 + 9
9 + 6	13	8 + 9
9 + 5	14	3 + 9
9 + 2	15	2 + 9
9 + 3	16	6 + 9
9 + 9	17	7 + 9
9 + 8	18	9 + 9

Circle the greater number in each pair.

| 39 | **92** | | **73** | 37 |

| 54 | 45 | | **82** | 28 |

| 78 | **87** | | **52** | 25 |

Color the rectangles. X the shapes that are not rectangles.

Lesson 20.3B

Complete the equations and sentences to match the word problems.

You have 9 donuts in one box.
You have 3 donuts in the other box.
How many donuts do you have in all?

_____ ◯ _____ = _____

_____

I have _____ donuts in all.

You have 9 donuts in one box.
You have 6 donuts in the other box.
How many donuts do you have in all?

_____ ◯ _____ = _____

_____

I have _____ donuts in all.

You have 9 donuts in one box.
You have 5 donuts in the other box.
How many donuts do you have in all?

_____ ◯ _____ = _____

_____

I have _____ donuts in all.

Complete.

2 + 9 = _____   7 + 9 = _____

9 + 9 = _____   9 + 4 = _____

6 + 9 = _____   5 + 9 = _____

9 + 8 = _____   9 + 3 = _____

Complete the missing numbers on the 100 Chart.

____	16	17	____	19	____
25	26	27	____	29	30
35	____	37	____	39	40
____	46	47	____	49	50
55	56	57	____	59	____

See *Instructor Guide* for directions on how to play.
Save this game board for future lessons.

161

Adding 8s Crash
Game Board

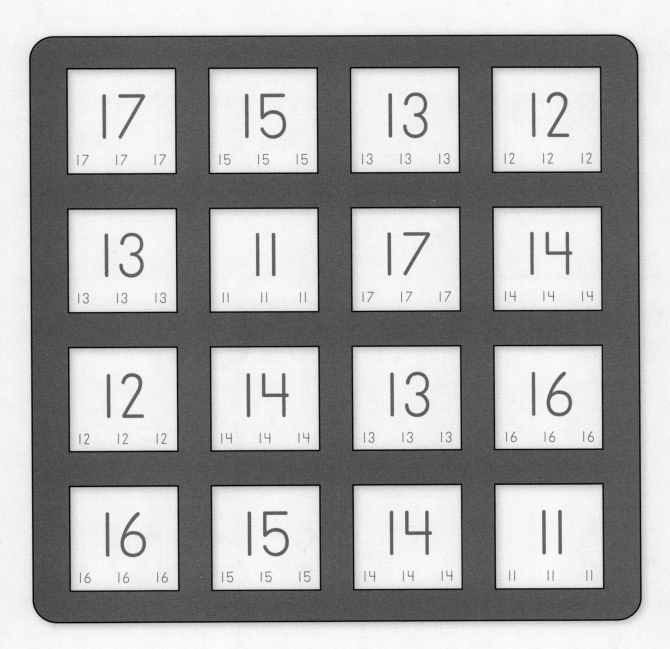

Complete.

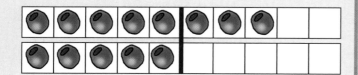

$8 + 5 = \underline{\hspace{2cm}}$

$8 + 7 = \underline{\hspace{2cm}}$

$8 + 2 = \underline{\hspace{2cm}}$

$8 + 8 = \underline{\hspace{2cm}}$

$8 + 3 = \underline{\hspace{2cm}}$

$8 + 6 = \underline{\hspace{2cm}}$

$8 + 4 = \underline{\hspace{2cm}}$

$8 + 9 = \underline{\hspace{2cm}}$

8 + 4	10	5 + 9
8 + 7	11	3 + 9
8 + 6	12	4 + 9
8 + 5	13	8 + 9
8 + 2	14	1 + 9
8 + 3	15	2 + 9
9 + 8	16	6 + 9
8 + 8	17	7 + 9

X the shape that doesn't belong in each row.

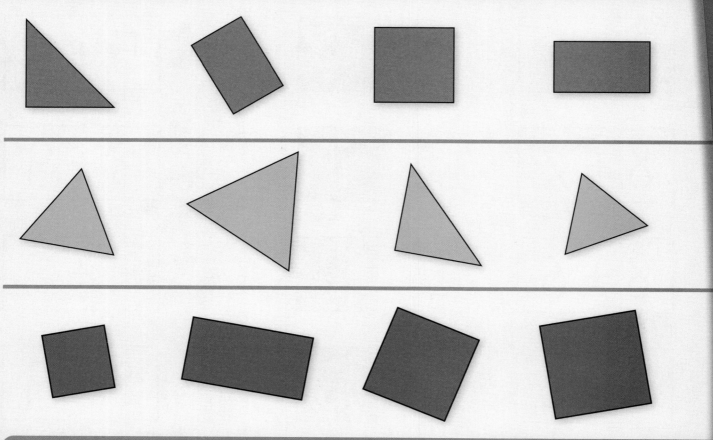

Connect the dots in order.

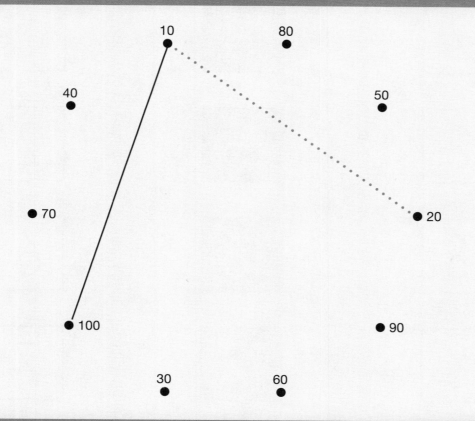

Lesson 21.2B

You have 8 blue balloons.
You have 3 yellow balloons.
How many balloons do you have?

_____ ◯ _____ = _____

I have _____ balloons.

You have 8 red balloons.
You have 7 yellow balloons.
How many balloons do you have?

_____ ◯ _____ = _____

I have _____ balloons.

You have 8 green balloons.
You have 6 yellow balloons.
How many balloons do you have?

_____ ◯ _____ = _____

I have _____ balloons.

3 + 8 = ⎯⎯⎯⎯

8 + 8 = ⎯⎯⎯⎯

9 + 8 = ⎯⎯⎯⎯

8 + 4 = ⎯⎯⎯⎯

6 + 8 = ⎯⎯⎯⎯

5 + 8 = ⎯⎯⎯⎯

8 + 7 = ⎯⎯⎯⎯

2 + 8 = ⎯⎯⎯⎯

Complete.

33 + 1 = ⎯⎯⎯⎯

33 + 10 = ⎯⎯⎯⎯

48 + 1 = ⎯⎯⎯⎯

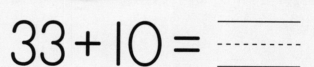

48 + 10 = ⎯⎯⎯⎯

25 + 1 = ⎯⎯⎯⎯

25 + 10 = ⎯⎯⎯⎯

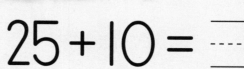

Complete.

10 + 1 = _____ 10 + 9 = _____

10 + 8 = _____ 0 + 8 = _____

7 + 0 = _____ 7 + 10 = _____

10 + 3 = _____ 2 + 10 = _____

Color the addition facts that equal the number in the star.

14

| 10 + 4 |
| 8 + 6 |
| 4 + 8 |
| 9 + 5 |

15

| 9 + 6 |
| 10 + 6 |
| 8 + 7 |
| 9 + 5 |

16

| 8 + 8 |
| 6 + 9 |
| 7 + 9 |
| 10 + 6 |

Maria made a tally chart of how many times she did her chores. Use the chart to answer the questions.

How many times did she set the table? _____

How many times did she make her bed? _____

How many times did she feed the dog? _____

Did she make her bed or set the table more times?

_____

_____

Chores Tally Chart

Set the table	IIII I
Make my bed	IIII II
Feed the dog	IIII IIII

Circle the squares that are split in half. X the squares that are not split in half.

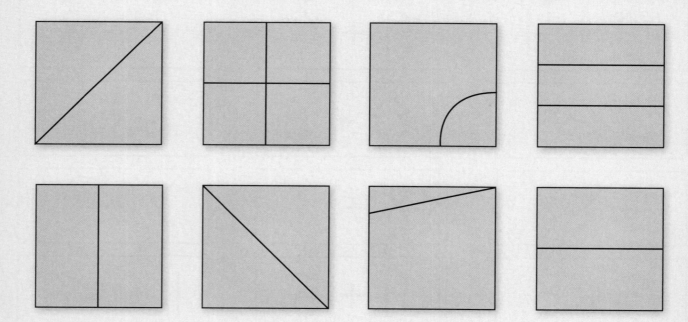

Lesson 21.4B

Addition Tic-Tac-Toe
Game Board

Complete.

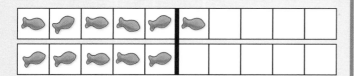

$$6 + 5 = \underline{\hspace{3cm}}$$

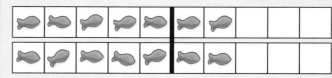

$$7 + 7 = \underline{\hspace{3cm}}$$

$$7 + 6 = \underline{\hspace{3cm}}$$

$$5 + 7 = \underline{\hspace{3cm}}$$

$$7 + 5 = \underline{\hspace{3cm}}$$

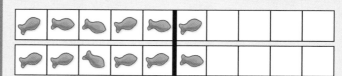

$$6 + 6 = \underline{\hspace{3cm}}$$

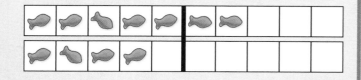

$$7 + 4 = \underline{\hspace{3cm}}$$

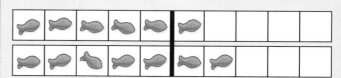

$$6 + 7 = \underline{\hspace{3cm}}$$

Complete.

5 + 6 = _____

6 + 7 = _____

7 + 7 = _____

6 + 6 = _____

5 + 7 = _____

6 + 5 = _____

7 + 6 = _____

4 + 7 = _____

Match.

7 + 6		5 + 8
8 + 7	13	8 + 6
4 + 9	14	5 + 9
7 + 7	15	9 + 6

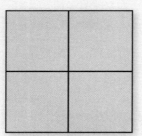
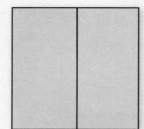

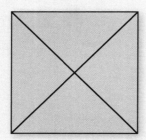
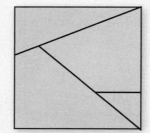
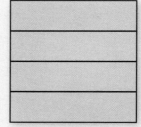

Circle the greater number in each pair.

30   32   77   70

56   65   8   18

8   80   9   11

You have 6 red apples.
You have 5 green apples.
How many apples do you have?

_____ ◯ _____ = _____

_____

I have _____ apples.

You have 6 red apples.
You have 6 green apples.
How many apples do you have?

_____ ◯ _____ = _____

_____

I have _____ apples.

You have 7 red apples.
You have 4 green apples.
How many apples do you have?

_____ ◯ _____ = _____

_____

I have _____ apples.

Complete.

$5 + 6 =$ _____

$6 + 7 =$ _____

$7 + 7 =$ _____

$6 + 6 =$ _____

$5 + 7 =$ _____

$6 + 5 =$ _____

$7 + 6 =$ _____

$4 + 7 =$ _____

Match pairs that make 100.

60	20
80	30
50	40
70	50

Color the addition facts that equal the number in the star.

11

| 6 + 5 |
| 8 + 2 |
| 4 + 7 |
| 9 + 1 |

12

| 7 + 6 |
| 3 + 9 |
| 4 + 8 |
| 8 + 2 |

13

| 5 + 8 |
| 9 + 3 |
| 7 + 7 |
| 7 + 6 |

14

| 7 + 7 |
| 9 + 4 |
| 6 + 8 |
| 5 + 7 |

15

| 9 + 6 |
| 8 + 7 |
| 4 + 8 |
| 8 + 8 |

16

| 9 + 9 |
| 8 + 8 |
| 6 + 5 |
| 7 + 9 |

Match.

$90 + 5$	71
$50 + 3$	17
$70 + 1$	95
$30 + 5$	59
$50 + 9$	53
$10 + 7$	35

Draw a congruent shape.

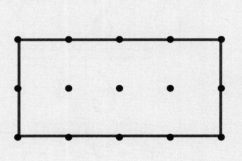

Complete the missing dates.

MARCH

Sunday	Monday	Tuesday	Wednesday	Thursday	Friday	Saturday
		1	_____	3	4	5
_____	7	8	9	10	_____	12
13	14	15	16	_____	18	19
20	_____	22	23	24	25	_____
27	28	29	_____	31		

Use the calendar to answer the questions.

What day of the week is March 4? _____

What day of the week is March 25? _____

What day of the week is March 20? _____

What day of the week is March 29? _____

Complete.

9 + 4 = _____   6 + 8 = _____

8 + 7 = _____   5 + 7 = _____

7 + 10 = _____   8 + 8 = _____

4 + 9 = _____   4 + 5 = _____

Trace.

1 foot = 12 inches

Draw a line of symmetry for each shape.

Trace.

1 year = <u>12</u> months

1 week = <u>7</u> days

1 day = <u>24</u> hours

1 hour = <u>60</u> minutes

1 minute = <u>60</u> seconds

Match.

10:00	9 o'clock
4:00	6 o'clock
9:00	4 o'clock
6:00	12 o'clock
12:00	10 o'clock

Complete.

$9 + 5 =$ _____ $6 + 6 =$ _____

$8 + 4 =$ _____ $9 + 7 =$ _____

$30 + 40 =$ _____ $30 + 4 =$ _____

$45 + 10 =$ _____ $45 + 1 =$ _____

Complete the number patterns.

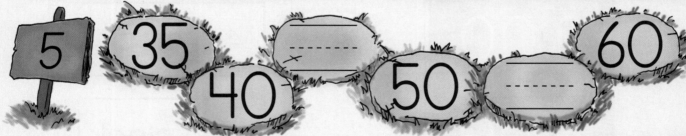

Match.

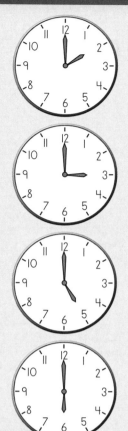

5:00

10:00

2:00

6:00

3:00

Write the time.

7:00

Complete.

10 − 7 = _____   9 − 5 = _____

8 − 4 = _____   8 − 2 = _____

9 − 6 = _____   10 − 5 = _____

7 − 3 = _____   6 − 5 = _____

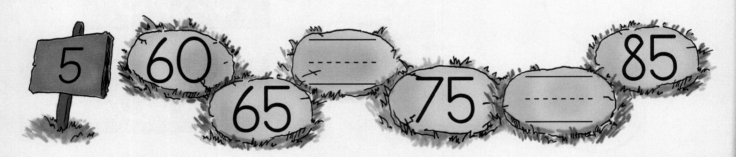

5   60   _____   85

65   75   _____

Complete the equation and sentence to match the word problem.

You have 9 cookies.
4 have yellow frosting.
The rest have green frosting.
How many have green frosting?

_____ ◯ _____ = _____

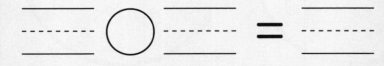

_____ cookies have green frosting.

Match.

12:30

1:30

5:30

7:30

9:30

Write the time.

2:30

9 + 6 = _____   6 + 5 = _____

8 + 3 = _____   7 + 7 = _____

60 + 20 = _____   60 + 2 = _____

85 + 10 = _____   85 + 1 = _____

Emma made a bar graph of the books she checked out from the library. Use the bar graph to answer the questions.

My Library Books

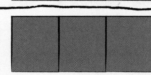

Poetry

Fairy Tales

Science

How many fairy tale books did she check out? _____

How many science books did she check out? _____

Did she check out more science or fairy tale books? _____

How many more? _____

$ _____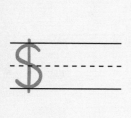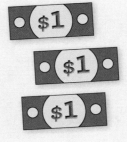

$ _____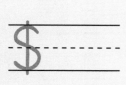

$ _____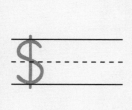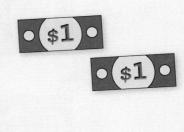

$ _____

9 + 3 = _____   6 + 6 = _____

8 + 4 = _____   9 + 7 = _____

9 + 10 = _____   8 + 8 = _____

5 + 9 = _____   6 + 5 = _____

Match pairs that make 100.

10		60
20		90
30		70
40		80

Circle the greater number of dollars.

 $39 $9 | $93  $39

$40 $39 | $3 $39

$39 $38 | $30 $39

Complete.

$ _____   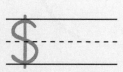 $10 $10 $10 $5 $5 $5 $5    $1 $1 $1 $1 $1

$ _____    $10 $10 $10 $10 $10    $5 $5 $5    $1

Complete.

9 + 7 = _____   6 + 6 = _____

8 + 5 = _____   4 + 7 = _____

50+50 = _____   50 + 5 = _____

67+10 = _____   67 + 1 = _____

Write the time.

7:00

_____

_____

7:30

_____

_____

Match.

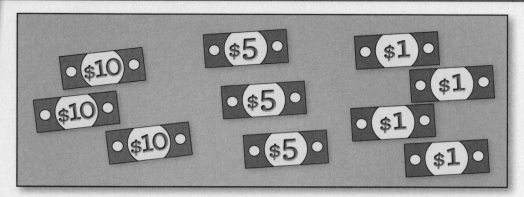

$75

$70

$61

$49

Complete.

10 − 6 = _____   10 − 9 = _____

8 − 7 = _____   9 − 3 = _____

8 − 3 = _____   8 − 4 = _____

9 − 2 = _____   7 − 6 = _____

Complete or trace.

1 year = _____ months

1 week = _____ days

1 day = 24 hours

1 hour = 60 minutes

1 minute = 60 seconds

You have $40.
Then, you earn $20 more.
How much do you have now?

_____ ◯ _____ = _____

I have $_____ .

You have $35.
Then, you earn $10 more.
How much do you have now?

_____ ◯ _____ = _____

I have $_____ .

You have $26.
Then, you earn $1 more.
How much do you have now?

_____ ◯ _____ = _____

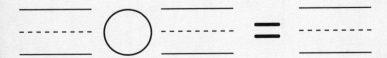

I have $_____ .

9 + 2 = -------   6 + 8 = -------

8 + 8 = -------   6 + 7 = -------

30 + 50 = -------   30 + 5 = -------

79 + 10 = -------   79 + 1 = -------

Write the time.

8:00

Complete.

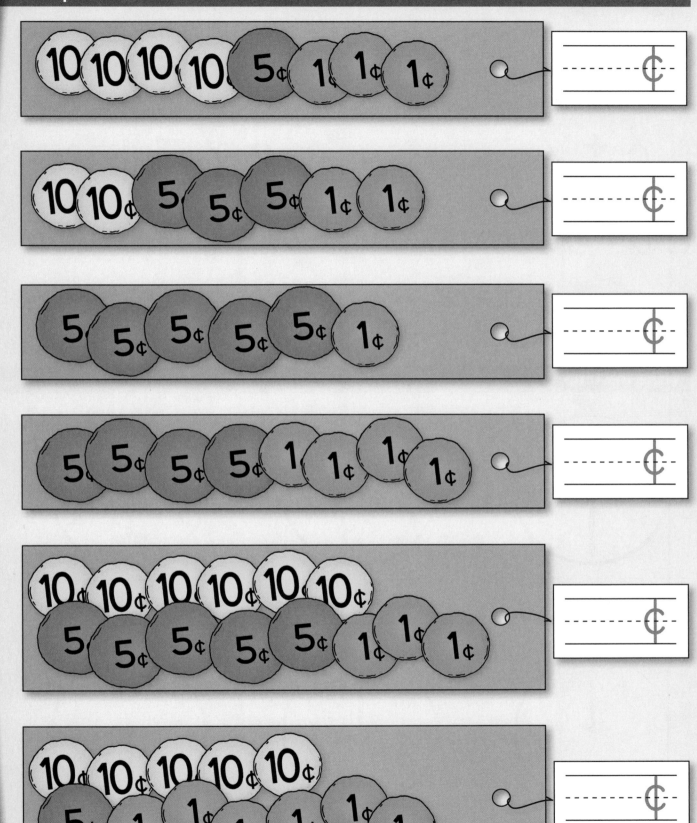

Complete.

9 + 9 = ----------

6 + 7 = ----------

8 + 7 = ----------

3 + 7 = ----------

1 + 10 = ----------

5 + 8 = ----------

2 + 9 = ----------

3 + 5 = ----------

Write the time.

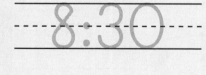
8:30

Complete.

_____ ¢

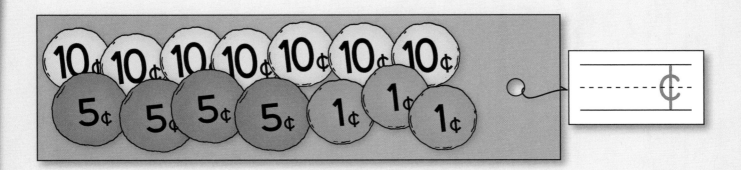

_____ ¢

_____ ¢

_____ ¢

$9 - 7 =$ _____ $10 - 5 =$ _____

$9 - 3 =$ _____ $8 - 7 =$ _____

$10 - 7 =$ _____ $8 - 4 =$ _____

$7 - 5 =$ _____ $9 - 5 =$ _____

Complete.

1 foot = _____ inches

Complete the equation and sentence to match the word problem.

There are 8 flowers.
3 are red. The rest are yellow.
How many flowers are yellow?

_____ ◯ _____ = _____

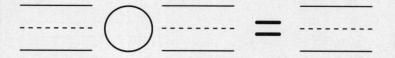

_____ flowers are yellow.

Complete.

10 − 6 = -------   7 − 3 = -------

8 − 6 = -------   9 − 1 = -------

8 − 5 = -------   9 − 8 = -------

10 − 2 = -------   7 − 4 = -------

Write the time.

9:30

You have 90¢.
Then, you spend 50¢.
How much money do you have now?

_____ ◯ _____ = _____

I have _____ ¢ .

You have 43¢.
Then, you earn 10¢ more.
How much do you have now?

_____ ◯ _____ = _____

I have _____ ¢ .

You have 43¢.
Then, you find 1¢ more.
How much do you have now?

_____ ◯ _____ = _____

I have _____ ¢ .

Complete.

$9 + 8 =$ _____ $6 + 9 =$ _____

$8 + 6 =$ _____ $4 + 7 =$ _____

$60 + 20 =$ _____ $60 + 2 =$ _____

$29 + 10 =$ _____ $29 + 1 =$ _____

Use a ruler to measure the ribbons in inches.

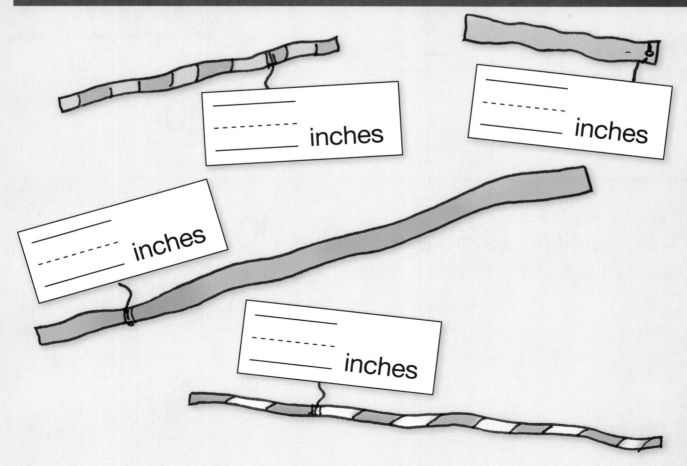

_____ inches

_____ inches

_____ inches

_____ inches

Subtraction Roll and Cover
Game Board

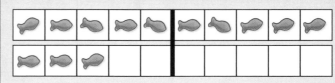

$$11 - 2 = \text{------}$$

$$13 - 4 = \text{------}$$

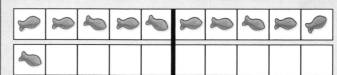

$$11 - 3 = \text{------}$$

$$11 - 5 = \text{------}$$

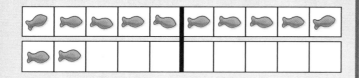

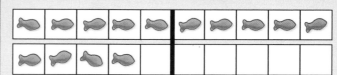

$$12 - 4 = \text{------}$$

$$14 - 5 = \text{------}$$

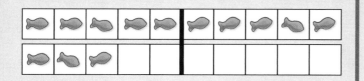

$$13 - 5 = \text{------}$$

$$12 - 3 = \text{------}$$

Complete. Use the ten-frames to help.

$$11 - 1 = \underline{}$$

$$11 - 2 = \underline{}$$

$$11 - 3 = \underline{}$$

$$11 - 4 = \underline{}$$

$$11 - 5 = \underline{}$$

$$12 - 1 = \underline{}$$

$$12 - 2 = \underline{}$$

$$12 - 3 = \underline{}$$

$$12 - 4 = \underline{}$$

$$12 - 5 = \underline{}$$

$$13 - 3 = \underline{}$$

$$13 - 4 = \underline{}$$

$$13 - 5 = \underline{}$$

$$14 - 3 = \underline{}$$

$$14 - 4 = \underline{}$$

$$14 - 5 = \underline{}$$

My Lunch

Cheese sandwich	▮▮▮▮▮
Peanut butter sandwich	▮▮▮▮▮▮
Ham sandwich	▮▮▮

How many times did he have a cheese sandwich?

_____

How many times did he have a peanut butter sandwich?

_____

How many times did he have a ham sandwich?

_____

How many more times did he have peanut butter than ham?

_____

How many more times did he have peanut butter than cheese?

_____

How many more times did he have cheese than ham?

_____

You have 13 stickers.
You use 5 stickers.
How many stickers are left?

_____ ◯ _____ = _____

_____

There are _____ stickers left.

You have 12 stickers.
4 are green. The rest are red.
How many stickers are red?

_____ ◯ _____ = _____

_____

_____ stickers are red.

You have 7 blue stickers and
6 orange stickers.
How many stickers do you have?

_____ ◯ _____ = _____

_____

I have _____ stickers.

Complete.

13 − 4 = _____

11 − 3 = _____

12 − 5 = _____

11 − 4 = _____

13 − 5 = _____

12 − 3 = _____

14 − 5 = _____

11 − 5 = _____

12 − 4 = _____

11 − 2 = _____

Write the time.

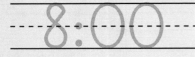
8:00

_____

_____

_____

_____

_____

Complete the fact families to match the Part-Total Diagrams.

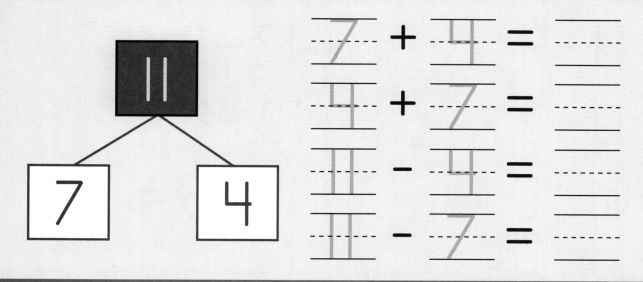

$$7 + 4 = $$
$$4 + 7 = $$
$$11 - 4 = $$
$$11 - 7 = $$

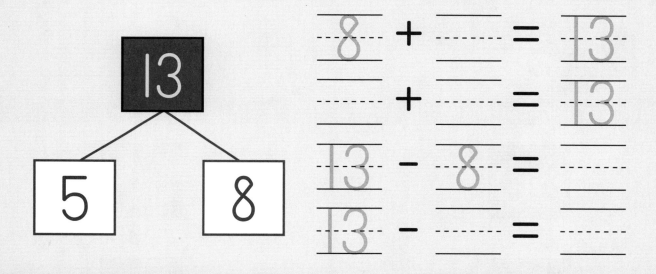

$$8 + \underline{} = 13$$
$$\underline{} + \underline{} = 13$$
$$13 - 8 = $$
$$13 - \underline{} = $$

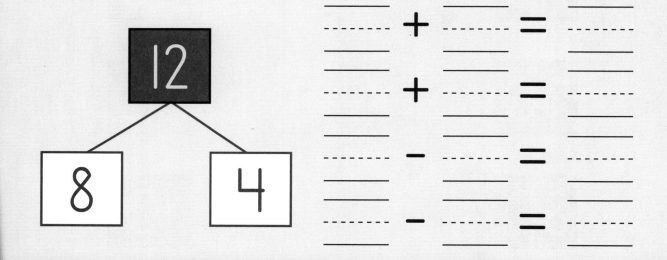

$$\underline{} + \underline{} = $$
$$\underline{} + \underline{} = $$
$$\underline{} - \underline{} = $$
$$\underline{} - \underline{} = $$

Complete.

11 − 4 = _____

12 − 3 = _____

11 − 2 = _____

13 − 5 = _____

11 − 5 = _____

14 − 5 = _____

12 − 4 = _____

13 − 4 = _____

12 − 5 = _____

11 − 3 = _____

Match the pairs that make 100.

50

30

70

20

90

50

80

10

Subtraction Bingo
Game Boards

B	I	N	G	O
4	5	7	3	6
6	2	8	4	9
9	7	FREE	8	2
3	5	6	5	7
8	4	2	9	3

B	I	N	G	O
5	3	8	7	3
8	2	7	4	6
4	6	FREE	9	5
7	9	3	8	2
2	4	6	5	9

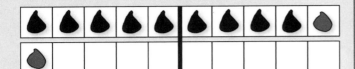

$9 +$ _____ $= 11$

$11 - 9 =$ _____

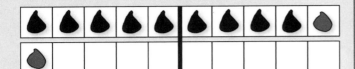

$9 +$ _____ $= 15$

$15 - 9 =$ _____

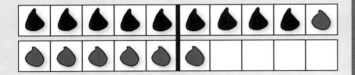

$9 +$ _____ $= 16$

$16 - 9 =$ _____

$9 +$ _____ $= 12$

$12 - 9 =$ _____

$9 +$ _____ $= 13$

$13 - 9 =$ _____

$9 +$ _____ $= 18$

$18 - 9 =$ _____

Complete the equations and sentences to match the word problems.

You have 13 green jelly beans.
You have 9 yellow jelly beans.
How many more are green?

13 ◯(-) 9 = _____

There are _____ more green jelly beans than yellow.

You have 9 orange jelly beans.
You have 14 purple jelly beans.
How many more are purple?

_____ ◯ _____ = _____

There are _____ more purple jelly beans than orange.

You have 12 red jelly beans.
You have 9 pink jelly beans.
How many more are red?

_____ ◯ _____ = _____

There are _____ more red jelly beans than pink.

Complete.

$12 - 9 =$ _____ $15 - 9 =$ _____

$14 - 9 =$ _____ $11 - 9 =$ _____

$18 - 9 =$ _____ $13 - 9 =$ _____

$17 - 9 =$ _____ $16 - 9 =$ _____

Match.

$12 - 4$		$11 - 3$
	7	
$11 - 2$		$13 - 5$
	8	
$12 - 5$		$14 - 5$
	9	
$13 - 4$		$11 - 4$

$8 +$ _____ $= 11$

$8 +$ _____ $= 14$

$11 - 8 =$ _____

$14 - 8 =$ _____

$8 +$ _____ $= 16$

$8 +$ _____ $= 12$

$16 - 8 =$ _____

$12 - 8 =$ _____

$8 +$ _____ $= 13$

$8 +$ _____ $= 15$

$13 - 8 =$ _____

$15 - 8 =$ _____

80 + 7	87
40 + 2	73
70 + 3	25
20 + 5	99
90 + 9	42

Complete.

$13 - 9 =$ _____ $12 - 9 =$ _____

$14 - 9 =$ _____ $15 - 9 =$ _____

$16 - 9 =$ _____ $18 - 9 =$ _____

$11 - 9 =$ _____ $17 - 9 =$ _____

11 − 8	2	15 − 9
15 − 8	3	17 − 9
13 − 8	4	18 − 9
16 − 8	5	11 − 9
17 − 8	6	12 − 9
12 − 8	7	14 − 9
14 − 8	8	16 − 9
	9	13 − 9

8:30

You have 37¢.
Then, you earn 10¢ more.
How much do you have now?

◯ =

I have ____¢ .

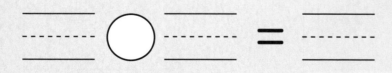

Connect the Boxes
Game Board

7	11 – 6	16 – 7	4	13 – 7
12 – 7	8	6	14 – 6	9
5	15 – 6	7	15 – 7	8
6	6	13 – 6	5	11 – 7
13 – 7	14 – 7	8	9	12 – 6

11 – 6 = _____

11 – 7 = _____

15 – 6 = _____

15 – 7 = _____

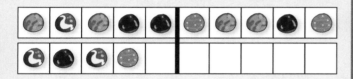

14 – 6 = _____

14 – 7 = _____

12 – 6 = _____

12 – 7 = _____

13 – 6 = _____

13 – 7 = _____

16 – 6 = _____

16 – 7 = _____

Complete the fact family to match.

12

7   5

```
....... + ....... = .......

....... + ....... = .......

....... - ....... = .......

....... - ....... = .......
```

Color the addition facts that equal the number in the star.

7

| 13 − 6 |
| 15 − 8 |
| 12 − 9 |
| 11 − 4 |
| 14 − 7 |

8

| 13 − 4 |
| 16 − 8 |
| 14 − 6 |
| 11 − 6 |
| 15 − 7 |

9

| 15 − 6 |
| 12 − 8 |
| 16 − 7 |
| 18 − 9 |
| 13 − 7 |

Match pairs that make 20.

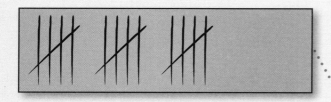

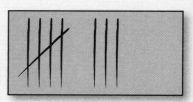

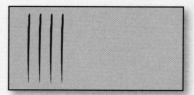

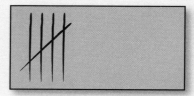

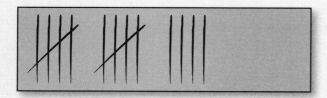

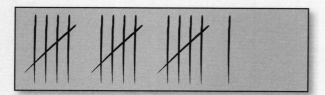

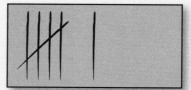

Draw a congruent shape.

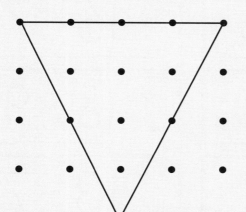

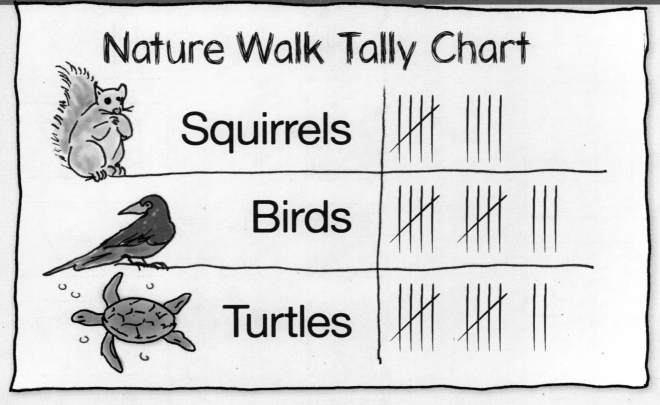

Tommy saw 9 squirrels and 13 birds.
How many more birds than squirrels did he see?

_____ ◯ _____ = _____

He saw _____ more birds than squirrels.

Tommy saw 9 squirrels and 12 turtles.
How many more turtles than squirrels did he see?

_____ ◯ _____ = _____

He saw _____ more turtles than squirrels.

Match.

$14 - 6$	**4**	$11 - 7$
$11 - 6$	**5**	$13 - 7$
$13 - 6$	**6**	$16 - 7$
$12 - 6$	**7**	$15 - 7$
$15 - 6$	**8**	$12 - 7$
	9	$14 - 7$

Write the time.

Complete the equations and sentences to match the word problems.

You have 12 brown eggs.
You have 7 white eggs.
How many more
are brown?

_____ (−) _____ = _____

There are _____ more brown eggs than white.

You have 6 brown eggs.
You have 13 white eggs.
How many more
are white?

_____ ( ) _____ = _____

There are _____ more white eggs than brown.

You have 8 brown eggs.
You have 9 white eggs.
How many eggs do
you have?

_____ ( ) _____ = _____

You have _____ eggs.

14 − 6 = _____   11 − 7 = _____

13 − 7 = _____   16 − 7 = _____

13 − 6 = _____   11 − 5 = _____

14 − 7 = _____   12 − 7 = _____

15 − 7 = _____   15 − 6 = _____

11 − 6 = _____   12 − 6 = _____

Use the key to color the sand pails.

Key
6 - green
7 - blue
8 - yellow

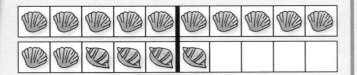

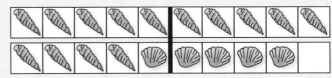

2 + 4 = _____

12 + 4 = _____

4 + 5 = _____

14 + 5 = _____

7 + 2 = _____

17 + 2 = _____

5 + 5 = _____

15 + 5 = _____

3 + 4 = _____

13 + 4 = _____

3 + 5 = _____

13 + 5 = _____

6 + 2 = _____

16 + 2 = _____

1 + 8 = _____

11 + 8 = _____

Complete the equation and sentence to match the word problem.

You have 13 square blocks.
You have 9 triangle blocks.
How many more are squares?

$$\underline{\quad\quad} \bigcirc \underline{\quad\quad} = \underline{\quad\quad}$$

There are _____ more squares than triangles.

Complete.

$$1 \text{ foot} = \underline{\quad\quad} \text{ inches}$$

Color the squares. X the shapes that are not squares.

Write the sum of each row of cards.

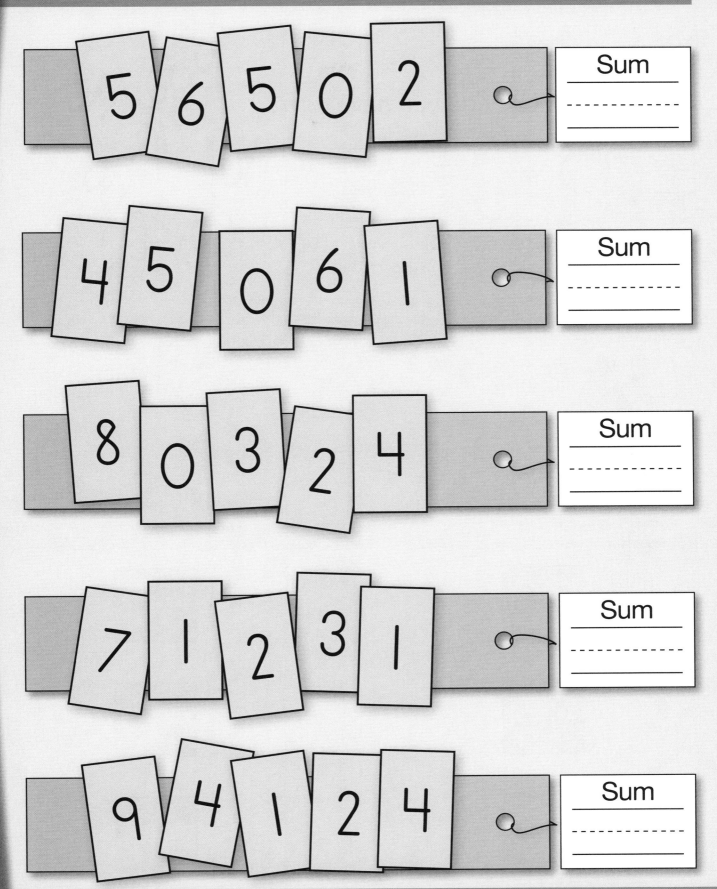

5 6 5 0 2 Sum _____

4 5 0 6 1 Sum _____

8 0 3 2 4 Sum _____

7 1 2 3 1 Sum _____

9 4 1 2 4 Sum _____

You have 80¢.
Then, you spend 30¢.
How much money do you have now?

_____ ◯ _____ = _____

I have _____ ¢ .

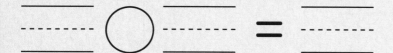

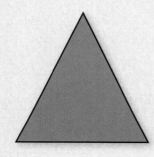

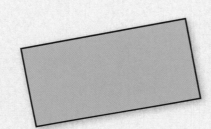

 40   50

 50   30

70   60

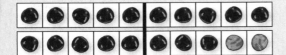

18 + 2 = _____

17 + 6 = _____

16 + 8 = _____

18 + 7 = _____

15 + 5 = _____

19 + 4 = _____

18 + 4 = _____

17 + 3 = _____

Cassie made a tally chart of the weather each day.
Use the chart to complete the equations and sentences.

Weather Tally Chart

☀ Sunny Days	‖‖‖ ‖‖‖ ‖‖‖
☁ Cloudy Days	‖‖‖ ‖‖‖
🌧 Rainy Days	‖‖‖ ‖‖

There were 14 sunny days and 9 cloudy days.
How many more sunny days than cloudy days were there?

_____ ◯ _____ = _____

There were _____ more sunny days than cloudy days.

There were 14 sunny days and 7 rainy days.
How many more sunny days than rainy days were there?

_____ ◯ _____ = _____

There were _____ more sunny days than rainy days.

20 - 4 = ____

20 - 5 = ____

20 - 7 = ____

20 - 8 = ____

20 - 9 = ____

20 - 10 = ____

20 - 1 = ____

20 - 11 = ____

Write the time.

_____   _____   _____
- - - - - - - - - - - - - -   - - - - - - - - - - - - - -   - - - - - - - - - - - - - -
_____   _____   _____

Draw lines that split each cake into fourths.

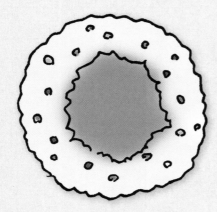 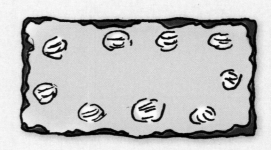

Complete the equation and sentence to match the word problem.

You have 13 crackers.
You eat 6 crackers.
How many crackers are left?

_____ ◯ _____ = _____

There are _____ crackers left.

Complete.

$27 + \underline{\hphantom{xxx}} = 30$

$35 + \underline{\hphantom{xxx}} = 40$

$46 + \underline{\hphantom{xxx}} = 50$

$31 + \underline{\hphantom{xxx}} = 40$

Complete. Look for a pattern in each column.

$50 + \underline{\hphantom{xxx}} = 50$

$30 + \underline{\hphantom{xxx}} = 40$

$49 + \underline{\hphantom{xxx}} = 50$

$31 + \underline{\hphantom{xxx}} = 40$

$48 + \underline{\hphantom{xxx}} = 50$

$32 + \underline{\hphantom{xxx}} = 40$

$47 + \underline{\hphantom{xxx}} = 50$

$33 + \underline{\hphantom{xxx}} = 40$

$46 + \underline{\hphantom{xxx}} = 50$

$34 + \underline{\hphantom{xxx}} = 40$

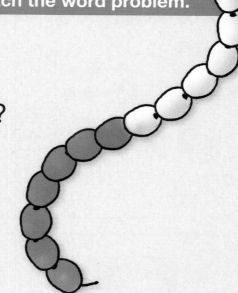

You put 7 green beads and
6 white beads on a string.
How many beads are on the string?

_____ ⃝ _____ = _____

I have _____ beads.

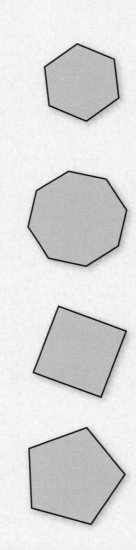

Complete.

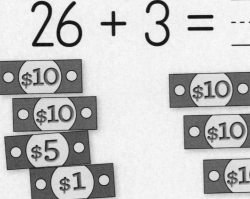

$17 + 2 =$ _____

$17 + 20 =$ _____

$31 + 2 =$ _____

$31 + 20 =$ _____

$26 + 3 =$ _____

$26 + 30 =$ _____

$40 + 3 =$ _____

$40 + 30 =$ _____

Draw a line of symmetry for each shape.

Complete the equation and sentence to match the word problem.

You have 14 erasers.
6 are purple. The rest are green.
How many erasers are green?

_____ ◯ _____ = _____

There are _____ green erasers.

Write the sum of each row of cards.

8 4 3 1 2

Sum
_____

7 5 0 3 5

Sum
_____

$27 + 4 =$ _____ $25 + 9 =$ _____

$35 + 6 =$ _____ $39 + 3 =$ _____

$48 + 4 =$ _____ $47 + 3 =$ _____

$46 + 5 =$ _____ $49 + 6 =$ _____

Complete the equation and sentence to match the word problem. 30.3B

You have 15 square blocks.
You have 9 triangle blocks.
How many more are squares?

$$\underline{\hspace{2cm}} \bigcirc \underline{\hspace{2cm}} = \underline{\hspace{2cm}}$$

There are $\underline{\hspace{1.5cm}}$ more squares than triangles.

Circle the greater number in each pair.

   80   88

    87   6   60

5   15   45   73

238   Lesson 30.3B

$9 + 2 =$ _____

$19 + 2 =$ _____

$8 + 4 =$ _____

$28 + 4 =$ _____

$5 + 5 =$ _____

$45 + 5 =$ _____

$7 + 5 =$ _____

$57 + 5 =$ _____

$6 + 7 =$ _____

$76 + 7 =$ _____

$8 + 8 =$ _____

$38 + 8 =$ _____

$3 + 8 =$ _____

$63 + 8 =$ _____

$9 + 1 =$ _____

$99 + 1 =$ _____

1 year = _____ months

1 week = _____ days

1 day = _____ hours

1 hour = _____ minutes

1 minute = _____ seconds

Complete the fact family to match.

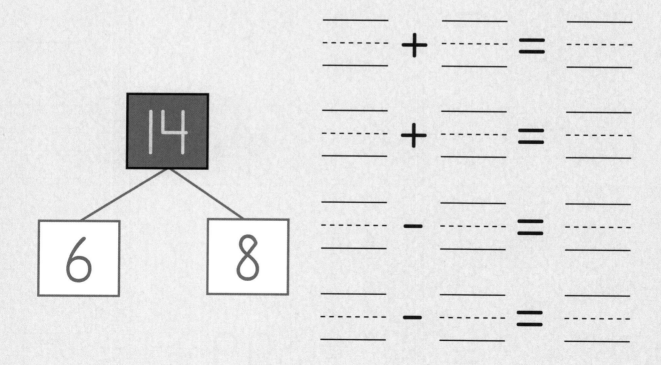

_____ + _____ = _____

_____ + _____ = _____

_____ - _____ = _____

_____ - _____ = _____

$37 - 1 =$ _____

$37 - 10 =$ _____

$53 - 3 =$ _____

$53 - 30 =$ _____

$49 - 4 =$ _____

$49 - 40 =$ _____

$34 - 2 =$ _____

$34 - 20 =$ _____

You put 6 beads on a string.
Then, you put 8 more beads on the string.
How many beads did you put on the string?

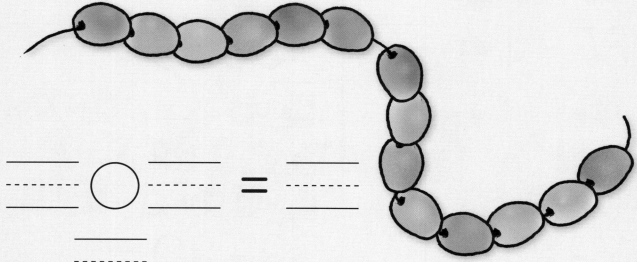

_____ ◯ _____ = _____

I put _____ beads on the string.

Complete.

_____ ¢

_____ ¢

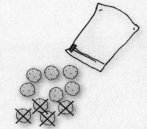

$30 - 4 =$ _____

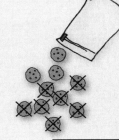

$30 - 7 =$ _____

$40 - 2 =$ _____

$40 - 8 =$ _____

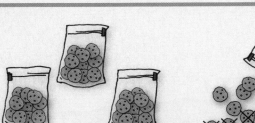

$40 - 5 =$ _____

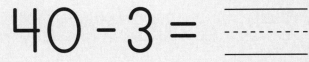

$40 - 3 =$ _____

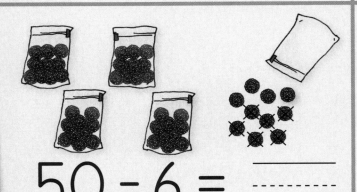

$50 - 6 =$ _____

$50 - 9 =$ _____

Use a ruler to measure the sticks in inches.

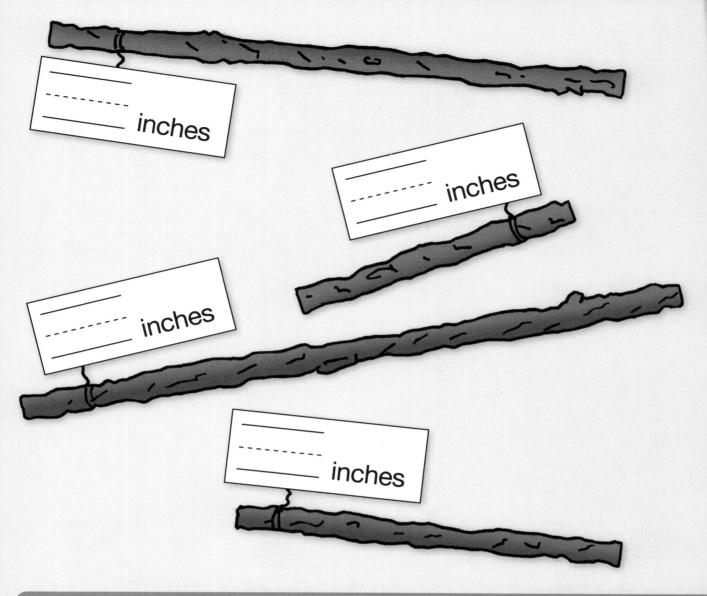

_____
- - - - - - -
_____ inches

_____
- - - - - - -
_____ inches

_____
- - - - - - -
_____ inches

_____
- - - - - - -
_____ inches

Copy the design.

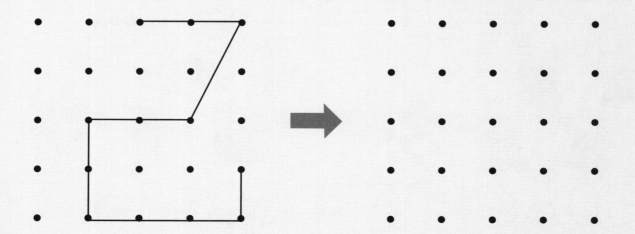

Lesson 31.2B

Complete. Look for a pattern in each column.

$10 - 5 =$ _____

$20 - 5 =$ _____

$30 - 5 =$ _____

$40 - 5 =$ _____

$50 - 5 =$ _____

$60 - 5 =$ _____

$70 - 5 =$ _____

$80 - 5 =$ _____

$90 - 5 =$ _____

$100 - 5 =$ _____

$10 - 1 =$ _____

$20 - 1 =$ _____

$30 - 1 =$ _____

$40 - 1 =$ _____

$50 - 1 =$ _____

$60 - 1 =$ _____

$70 - 1 =$ _____

$80 - 1 =$ _____

$90 - 1 =$ _____

$100 - 1 =$ _____

12 children are playing soccer.
5 are girls. The rest are boys.
How many are boys?

 =

There are _____ boys.

Match.

| 12:30 |

| 5:00 |

| 2:00 |

| 9:30 |

$40 - 1 =$ _____

$40 - 2 =$ _____

$40 - 3 =$ _____

$40 - 4 =$ _____

$40 - 5 =$ _____

$40 - 6 =$ _____

$40 - 7 =$ _____

$40 - 8 =$ _____

$40 - 9 =$ _____

$40 - 10 =$ _____

$90 - 1 =$ _____

$90 - 2 =$ _____

$90 - 3 =$ _____

$90 - 4 =$ _____

$90 - 5 =$ _____

$90 - 6 =$ _____

$90 - 7 =$ _____

$90 - 8 =$ _____

$90 - 9 =$ _____

$90 - 10 =$ _____

Books I Read

Story books	
Information books	
Poetry	

How many story books did she read? _____

How many information books
did she read? _____

How many poetry books did she read? _____

How many more story books than
information books did she read? _____

How many more story books than
poetry books did she read? _____

How many more poetry books than
information books did she read? _____

Complete the missing numbers on the 100 Chart.

	36	37		39	40
45		47		49	
55	56		58	59	60
	66		68	69	

Match pairs that make 100.

40   30

70   20

10   60

80   90

Match.

30 + 7 ⋯⋯⋯⋯

50 + 1

90 + 3

10 + 5

15

51

37

93

Complete the number patterns.

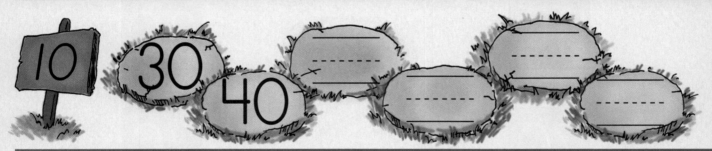

10 | 30 | 40 | ___ | ___ | ___ | ___

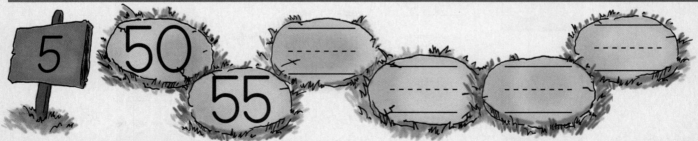

5 | 50 | 55 | ___ | ___ | ___ | ___

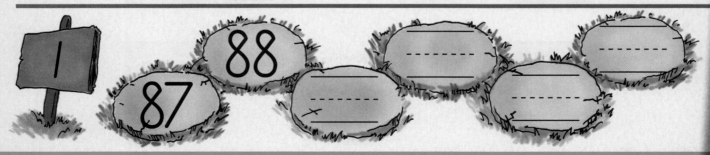

1 | 87 | 88 | ___ | ___ | ___ | ___

Match.

7 + 7		4 + 9
	13	
8 + 5		7 + 8
	14	
6 + 7		5 + 9
	15	
9 + 6		8 + 6

Complete.

$8 + 8 = \underline{\hspace{2cm}}$ $5 + 6 = \underline{\hspace{2cm}}$

$9 + 9 = \underline{\hspace{2cm}}$ $4 + 8 = \underline{\hspace{2cm}}$

$6 + 6 = \underline{\hspace{2cm}}$ $8 + 9 = \underline{\hspace{2cm}}$

$3 + 9 = \underline{\hspace{2cm}}$ $9 + 7 = \underline{\hspace{2cm}}$

Match pairs that make 20.

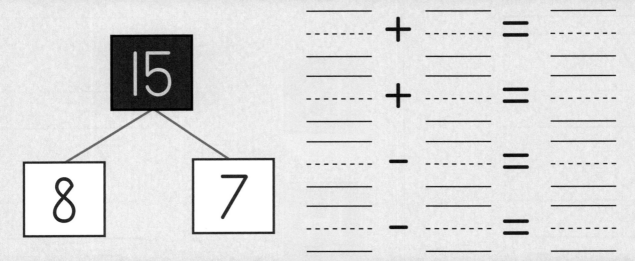

Color the subtraction facts that equal the number in the star.

★ 6	★ 7	★ 8
14 – 7	11 – 4	16 – 8
12 – 6	14 – 7	17 – 9
12 – 5	12 – 4	12 – 3
15 – 9	13 – 5	11 – 4
13 – 7	15 – 8	15 – 7

Lesson 32.2B

Use a ruler to measure the ribbons in inches.

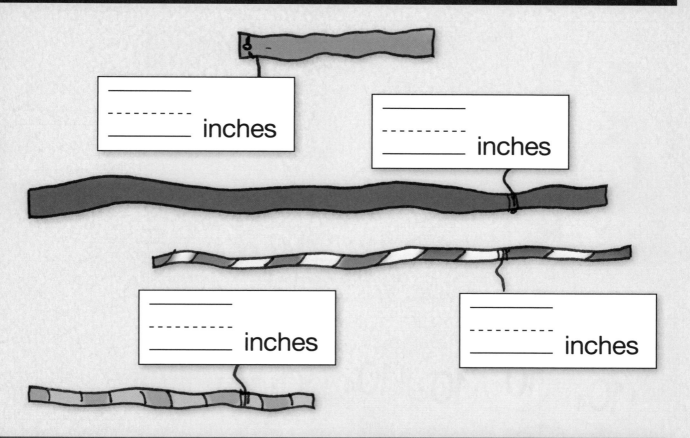

_____

- - - - - - - - -

_____ inches

_____

- - - - - - - - -

_____ inches

_____

- - - - - - - - -

_____ inches

_____

- - - - - - - - -

_____ inches

Draw a picture with a circle, square, and triangle.

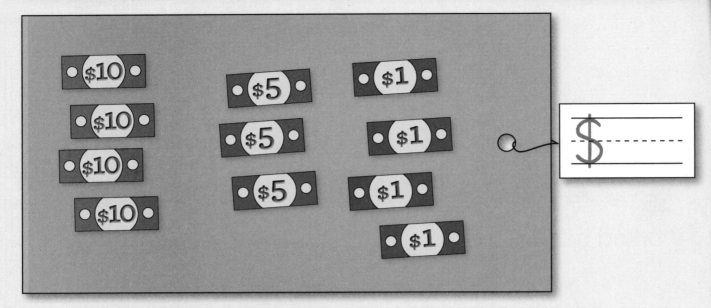

$ _____

_____ ¢

Write the time.

_____

_____

_____

Complete each sentence.

My favorite math activity this year was

_____

- -

_____

The most interesting thing I learned in math this year was

_____

- -

_____

I worked hard to learn

_____

- -

_____

Next year in math, I hope to learn

_____

- -

_____

Draw a picture of your favorite math activity from this year.

CONGRATULATIONS!

Presented to

_____

for successfully completing

First Grade Math
with Confidence

_____   _____

Date   Signature